Contents

During the financial year 1998–9 the Energy and Environmental Programme was supported by generous contributions of finance and technical advice from the following organizations:

Amerada Hess
BG
Blue Circle Industries
British Nuclear Fuels
British Petroleum
Eastern Electricity
ENI
Enron
Esso/Exxon
LASMO
Mitsubishi Fuels
Mobil Services
Osaka Gas
PowerGen
Ruhrgas
Saudi Aramco
Shell
Statoil
Tokyo Electric Power
Texaco
Veba Oil

Finance for this project was received from:

European Commission (DGI and DGXI)
German Ministry of the Environment

International Trade and Climate Change Policies

Duncan Brack with
Michael Grubb and Craig Windram

THE ROYAL INSTITUTE OF
INTERNATIONAL AFFAIRS
Energy and Environmental Programme

Earthscan Publications Ltd, London

First published in the UK in 2000 by
Royal Institute of International Affairs, 10 St James's Square, London, SW1Y 4LE
(Charity Registration No 208 223)
and
Earthscan Publications Ltd, 120 Pentonville Road London, N1 9JN

Distributed in North America by
The Brookings Institution, 1775 Massachusetts Ave NW,
Washington DC 20036–2188

A catalogue record for this book is available from the British Library

ISBN: 1 85383 620 6 paperback ✓

Typesetting by Composition & Design Services, Minsk, Belarus
Printed and bound by Creative Print and Design (Wales)
Cover design by Yvonne Booth

The Royal Institute of International Affairs is an independent body which promotes the rigorous study of international questions and does not express opinions of its own. The opinions expressed in this publication are the responsibility of the author

Earthscan is an editorially independent subsidiary of Kogan Page Limited and publishes in association with WWF-UK and the International Institute for Environment and Development

This book is printed on elemental chlorine free paper

List of figures, tables and boxes

Figures

Tables

Boxes

About the authors

Duncan Brack has been Head of the Energy and Environmental Programme (EEP) at the Royal Institute of International Affairs (RIIA), Chatham House, since September 1998. His work focuses on the interaction between trade and environmental issues, particularly on multilateral environmental agreements. He is currently working on a project on the growth and control of international environmental crime.

Michael Grubb was Head of EEP from January 1993 until September 1998. He is well known for his work on the policy implications of climate change. He is an adviser to a number of international organizations and studies, particularly concerning economic and policy aspects of climate change, and has been a lead author on a number of studies for the Intergovernmental Panel on Climate Change.

Craig Windram is the Director of E3 – Environment, Economics & Ethics – a strategic management consultancy and environmental think tank dedicated to making a business case for sustainable development. He is based in Brisbane, Australia, where he is currently working on a number of projects to commercialize alternative renewable energy technologies. He worked with EEP at RIIA for three months during 1998, focusing on climate change and trade issues.

Foreword

A critical challenge facing policy-makers in different parts of national administrations is to ensure consistency in the obligations they undertake in the many and varied international agreements under negotiation in the coming years. While this is no small task, the potential payoff is considerable, if at least one form of unnecessary international tension and conflict can be avoided. In this respect, few areas of international relations present a greater challenge than ensuring consistency between multilateral trade agreements and multilateral environment agreements.

Protecting the global commons – the planet's ozone layer, its biodiversity, endangered species, oceans and the temperature of the upper atmosphere – must be a top priority for all governments. Global problems require global solutions and these in turn require international cooperation and agreement. A number of critical multilateral environmental agreements will be negotiated in areas addressing subject matter as diverse as trade in genetically modified organisms and persistent organic pollutants. The conditions under which future generations live will in no small measure depend on the outcome of these negotiations.

On the other hand, a well functioning trading system based on multilaterally agreed rules rather than the power of individual trading nations is necessary to bring growth and stability to world trade in goods and services. Here too international agreement is of vital importance. While the existing rules governing international trade extend to not only goods but also trade in financial services, telecommunications, professional services, intellectual property rights and other areas, they may well be even further extended in the coming years to cover investment and competition policy. The manner in which world trade evolves – who produces what and where, and how the benefits are distributed – depends critically on the applications of these rules.

Environment and trade agreements represent two different bodies of international law, and their effective operation requires consistency between them. Serious conflicts can arise when measures taken in accordance with the legal obligation of one agreement violate those of another. The fact that there have been no disputes to date may well have led to misplaced complacency. The commercial and political importance, as well as the complexity, of some environment agreements dealing with transborder problems currently under negotiation has brought a new urgency to addressing the potential problems that may arise through a lack of coherence between the different bodies of law. On the trade side, the agreements are increasingly complex, of greater commercial significance and progressively extending their reach.

In this book, Duncan Brack and his colleagues address the interaction of two key driving forces of international relations in the modern world – trade liberalization and environment protection. In particular, they address the relationship between international trade policies and policies designed to mitigate climate change. They have chosen their topic well. Measures to deal with climate change, the Climate Change Convention itself and additional Protocols, along with measures affecting world trade and the World Trade Organization, represent regimes whose commercial, political and social significance is such that a lack of coherence between them will have serious implications on a global scale.

The timing of this book could not be better for policy-makers striving for coherence in both the trade and environment fields. While the United Nations Framework Convention entered into force on 21 March 1994, the specific provisions defining the nature of commitments by Members and legal instruments such as compliance procedures are to be elaborated in subsequent Protocols. In December 1997 the Kyoto Protocol to the Convention was adopted, the centre-piece being the commitments for developed countries to reduce their collective emission of greenhouse gases by at least 5 per cent by the period 2008–2012. In November 1998, the Buenos Aires Plan of Action was agreed to for finalizing the Protocol's outstanding details by the end of the year 2000. The negotiation of the mechanisms to implement the objectives of the climate change regime is at therefore a critical stage; there is time to ensure that whatever is agreed is coherent with the trade regime.

On the trade side, there is a growing body of opinion that a new round of multilateral trade negotiations will be launched in Seattle at the end of 1999. For a number of countries, ensuring a coherent relationship between multilateral trade and environment regimes will be a priority. For example in the communiqué from their meeting in Cologne in June 1999, the leaders of the G8 countries collectively called for a 'clarification of the relationship between both multilateral and environmental agreements and key environmental principles and WTO rules' in the next round of multilateral trade negotiations. In a similar vein, Sir Leon Brittan QC, in his former capacity as Vice President of the European Commission, expressed his concern with respect to the world trade rules and the climate change regime: 'Most of the governments that signed up to the Uruguay Round also accepted the outcome of Kyoto. There is a clear need for policy coherence here, and we owe it to ourselves to ensure that we do not make our task more difficult by taking on obligations that are incompatible.'[1]

The critical question addressed in the book is whether there will be a clash of regimes. The answer of many may well be no. The Parties to the Convention are clearly cognizant of the fact that measures taken to address climate change problems can have important implications for international trade. The Convention specifically states, for example, that measures taken to combat climate change, including unilateral ones, should not constitute a means of arbitrary or unjustifiable discrimination or a disguised restriction on international trade. It does not provide for any specific trade-related environmental measures. The Kyoto Protocol provides further formal assurance that the intention is to avoid use of trade-distorting measures; parties shall strive to implement policies and measures 'in such a way to minimize adverse effects ... on international trade'; but it, too, does not provide for any trade measures.

One of Duncan Brack's most important contributions in this book is his assertion that notwithstanding the assurances, measures will be taken to mitigate climate change irrespective of what is specifically provided for in any multilateral conventions or protocols. He makes it clear that to achieve the emission reductions of the Kyoto Protocol, a

---

[1] See Leon Brittan, in Saddrudin Aga Khan (ed.), *Policing the Global Economy: Why, How and for Whom?* (London: Cameron and May, 1998).

wide variety of measures will be taken that will certainly affect the costs of production and the competitive position of producers in the world market. Offsetting measures will be called for by those whose competitive position is adversely affected by cheaper imports not subject to the same measures in the country of origin. The book addresses two important and clearly interrelated questions. Are the measures taken to address climate change concerns protectionist in intent and do they violate WTO rules? In other words, will there be a clash of regimes?

As the author notes, at this stage at least, the climate change agreements contain no specific details on the precise nature of either the domestic measures to implement emission reductions or the flexibility mechanisms. In fact, their description of the domestic measures that may be taken to achieve the objectives of the climate change agreement is particularly vague. The Protocol states that in achieving their emission reduction commitments, Parties shall implement certain policies and measures, and then provides a general description of them. For example, to promote sustainable development, Parties shall elaborate policies or measures to enhance energy efficiency, protect and enhance carbon sinks and reservoirs, promote research and development and the application of market instruments, increase the use of new and renewable forms of energy and environmentally sound technologies, and phase out fiscal incentives and exemptions in greenhouse gas-emitting sectors. They may well affect the costs of production of traded goods and therefore the competitive position of producers in the world market. Energy, carbon and other taxes, mandatory and voluntary standards, subsidies for environmentally friendly production processes, labelling and certification schemes and the sale and transfer of emission permits within or between groups of countries all provide examples that are discussed in the book. They – and other measures – are examined in the light of their consistency with trade rules. The author also notes that offsetting measures will be called for by those whose competitive position is adversely affected by cheaper imports not subject to the same measures in the country of origin. He usefully addresses whether there is the potential for such taxes and other measures to be inconsistent with trade rules.

A recurring theme in the book is that measures that could be taken to mitigate climate change may well challenge some of the most fundamental trade principles. One particular example relates to production processes and their regulation. As the author explains, trade rules do not inhibit governments from taxing as they wish the production and consumption of products produced within national boundaries. Similarly, there are no problems from a trade perspective with governments regulating according to the manner in which a product is produced within their territory. There can, for example, be domestic taxes on production methods that are directed to reducing energy consumption or greenhouse gas emissions. The important point is, however that this flexibility only extends to regulation of domestically produced or imported products and domestic production processes. It does not extend to flexibility in the application of measures relating to production processes in exporting countries. The far-reaching implications of this approach are systematically dealt with under several headings in the book, such as border tax adjustment, labelling schemes and technical standards.

Duncan Brack also addresses the fact the many of the mechanisms that have emerged as tools to combat climate change are new and untried on a global scale. There is, for example, the possibility of Parties acting within bubbles to jointly achieve their emission reduction commitments. Countries adopting this procedure will have met their reduction commitments if their total aggregate emissions do not exceed the total of their combined amounts. Novel measures and schemes are most likely to be introduced to implement emissions reductions – in particular, an international 'emissions trading' regime allowing industrialized countries to buy and sell emissions credits among themselves. The author usefully analyses the possible implications of such a regime in the light of existing trade rules, as well as the 'clean development mechanism' which enables industrialized countries to finance emissions-reduction projects in developing countries and to receive credit for doing so.

In the broadest perspective, this book is about the fact that implementing measures to protect the global environment while ensuring a stable and predictable world trading system is a precondition for sus-

tainable development in the next millennium. What is required is a series of mutually supporting trade and environment agreements with
effective enforcement mechanisms for binding commitments undertaken by national governments. By presenting in a well-written and
accessible manner the potential implications of measures taken to mitigate climate change for the international trade regime, this book fills an
important gap that could not be more timely from a policy perspective.

Gary Sampson
Department of International Relations
London School of Economics

Acknowledgments

Many people have provided invaluable help and support to me in the rather long drawn-out preparation of this report. Pride of place must of course go to my co-authors, Michael Grubb (Chapter 2 and part of Chapter 3) and Craig Windram (parts of Chapters 1, 4, 6 and most of 5). Michael was also my former programme head in the Energy and Environmental Programme at Chatham House, and provided helpful supervision and oversight over most of the lifetime of the project, as did Benn Steil of the International Economics Programme.

The report would not have been published without financial assistance from the European Commission (DGI and DGXI) and the German Ministry of the Environment, who have all been good friends to the Energy and Environmental Programme for many years.

My thanks go to all the participants in the two Study Groups that were held to discuss various drafts of the report, and particularly to Hélène Cavé (European Commission, DGI) and Peter Horrocks and Julio Garcia-Burgues (DGXI) and several of their colleagues for additional comments.

A number of individuals at the International Institute for Energy Conservation, at both their US and UK offices, provided help with Chapter 3, and early drafts of Chapters 4, 6 and 7 were originally written as papers for conferences, organized respectively by IVM (Netherlands), IBC and the TMC Asser Instituut (Netherlands).

Ben Coles, Nikki Kerrigan and Matt Thomas of the Energy and Environmental Programme provided much-needed administrative and financial assistance, and Margaret May of Chatham House's Publications Department tolerated my complete inability to meet deadlines.

Finally, I would like to thank in particular Lucas Assunção, Penny Brooke, James Cameron, Jo Depledge, Fiona Mullins, Gary Sampson, Patrick Szell, Scott Vaughan, Jake Werksmann, Richard Westin and

Zhong Xiang Zhang; all have been immensely helpful above and beyond the call of duty. Final responsibility for the text of course remains with me.

Duncan Brack
August 1999

Abbreviations and acronyms

ACEA	Association des Constructeurs Européens d'Automobiles (European Automobile Manufacturers' Association)
AG13	Ad Hoc Group on Article 13 (of the FCCC)
BTA	border tax adjustment
CAFE	(US) Corporate Average Fuel Economy (regulations)
CDM	clean development mechanism
CER	certified emission reduction
CFCs	chlorofluorocarbons
CITES	Convention on International Trade in Endangered Species
CTE	(WTO) Committee on Trade and Environment
DGI	Directorate-General I (external relations) of the European Commission
DGXI	Directorate-General XI (environment, nuclear safety and civil protection) of the European Commission
FCCC	(United Nations) Framework Convention on Climate Change
GATS	General Agreement on Trade in Services
GATT	General Agreement on Tariffs and Trade
GPS	Global Positioning Systems
HFCs	hydrofluorocarbons
ICAO	International Civil Aviation Organization
IMO	International Maritime Organization
IPCC	Intergovernmental Panel on Climate Change
ISO	International Organization for Standardization
JAMA	Japan Automobile Manufacturers Association
JI	Joint Implementation
MAI	Multilateral Agreement on Investment
MARPOL	International Convention for the Prevention of Pollution from Ships

MEA	multilateral environmental agreement
MTS	multilateral trading system
NO_x	nitrogen oxides
ODC	ozone-depleting chemical
ODS	ozone-depleting substance
PFCs	perfluorocarbons
PPMs	process and production methods
SBSTA	(FCCC) Subsidiary Body for Scientific and Technical Advice
SCM	(WTO Agreement on) Subsidies and Countervailing Measures
SO_x	sulphur oxides
SPS	(WTO Agreement on) the Application of Sanitary and Phytosanitary Measures
TBT	(WTO Agreement on) Technical Barriers to Trade
TRIMS	(WTO Agreement on) Trade-related Investment Measures
TRIPS	(WTO Agreement on) Trade-related Aspects of Intellectual Property Rights
UNCED	United Nations Conference on Environment and Development
UNEP	United Nations Environment Programme
USTR	United States Trade Representative
VOC	volatile organic compounds
WMO	World Meteorological Organization
WTO	World Trade Organization

Summary and conclusions

This book is about one particular aspect of the interaction of two of the key driving forces of international relations in the modern world, trade liberalization and environmental protection. It deals with the relationship between international trade and policies designed to mitigate climate change. In particular, it explore the nature of the possible interactions between the requirements of the Kyoto Protocol, and policies and measures that are adopted in response to it, and international patterns of trade and their legal framework, the multilateral trading system (MTS) overseen by the World Trade Organization (WTO).

Trade impacts of climate change policies

Actions by industrialized countries to limit CO_2 emissions can affect other countries in several ways, including through impacts on international energy markets, trade in energy-intensive goods, overall trade structures and volumes, and reduced climatic impacts, particularly on agriculture. Economic modelling studies have sought to quantify the scale of the first three components, but at least for the level of commitments agreed at Kyoto that these probably exaggerate the scale of trade impacts.

Raising energy costs to energy-intensive manufacturing could result in these activities migrating to other countries, but precisely for that reason these sectors are likely to be shielded in one way or another. Reduced income in industrialized countries could reduce imports, but the models applied tend to neglect the scope for 'no-regret' measures that reduce emissions without reducing aggregate income. Also, many such models appear to exaggerate income-related trade impacts and do not take adequate account of recent trade liberalization, thus potentially underestimating the extent to which price responses may offset income effects on international trade. Also, economic modelling studies neglect the offsetting benefits of reducing climate change, which may be particularly important in terms of agricultural impacts on developing countries.

On time scales of 10 to 20 years, the effects on oil markets appear likely to dominate other mechanisms. This implies a small net economic gain in terms of trade for the majority of developing countries, with losses concentrated upon the countries which depend primarily on oil or coal exports. For the most part however, the effects of industrialized country action on other countries, both positive and negative, will be indistinguishable compared to the projected global growth in wealth and trade.

Energy efficiency standards and trade

The application of minimum standards of energy efficiency, and of labels showing energy consumption, is becoming more widespread in countries aiming to reduce energy demand and emissions of carbon dioxide. It would appear to be the case that at least current energy efficiency standards and labels, and their associated testing and certification systems, pose few if any barriers to trade. Trade barriers would be minimized, of course, by the harmonization of standards, but there are serious objections, including the facts that product standards are static instruments that can act to frustrate dynamic and innovative developments; standards will often need to vary with factors such as consumer preferences, climate or other national regulations; monitoring and enforcement costs could be significant; and the time and effort needed to negotiate standards on the part of policy-makers can be substantial. Given the potential for trade to spread higher standards, it seems logical to conclude that the costs of trying to agree common energy efficiency standards across any more than a small group of countries outweigh the benefits, though clearly the development and evolution of stronger *national* standards should be encouraged. There is a much stronger case, however, for attempting to harmonize labelling requirements and testing procedures, in order to reduce the bureaucracy and costs involved in exporting to different destinations. Energy efficiency regulations need to be applied in a non-discriminatory way to avoid clashes with the MTS – but there seems to be no environmental case for discrimination in this area.

Energy pricing and trade

Of all the issues examined in this book, the question of energy pricing policy – the application of energy and/or carbon taxes, and the use or withdrawal of subsidies for particular forms of energy production and use – and its role in climate change mitigation, is likely to trigger most controversy, raising key questions of international competitiveness.

Energy and carbon taxes have a valuable role to play in incorporating environmental externalities – chiefly, climate change – in prices and decision-making, and could usefully be deployed more extensively in more countries. Given the partly real, partly perceived concerns over the impact on international competitiveness, however, some combination of offsetting measures will be necessary. Revenue recycling, either through general reductions in other taxes and/or through targeted recycling for energy-intensive sectors, is hugely preferable to exemptions. In addition, border tax adjustments (probably restricted to a limited range of energy-intensive products and processes) may well prove to be of value, and their practicality should be explored. Subsidies can also be used to capture environmental externalities: those which act to increase greenhouse gas emissions (for example, for coal production) should be reduced and eventually eliminated; those which act to reduce them (for example, for renewable energy development) should be used more proactively.

The interaction of energy pricing policies with the MTS – particularly the WTO-legality of border tax adjustments, and of subsidies applied to reinforce climate change mitigation measures – must be explored and inconsistencies resolved.

International taxation of bunker fuels

The general trade-environment problem of failure to internalize environmental externalities applies in particular to transport, a major source of greenhouse gas emissions from the combustion of oil and its derivatives. This problem is exacerbated in the case of international aviation and marine 'bunker fuels' because of international agreements exempting them from taxation. However, the Kyoto Protocol instructs Annex I parties specifically to pursue the limitation or reduction of emissions of greenhouse gases from this source. Possible taxation of bunker fuels poses difficult questions of feasibility connected with the international scope and operations of the industries. The removal of their tax exemption would clearly be most effective if it is applied at a global level, but this is unlikely in the short term. Given this, and given the high levels of energy efficiency of marine transport and the high propensity of ship operators to move between different suppliers, there is very little advantage to be gained in seeking to apply sub-global taxation to marine bunker fuels. Given the much lower levels of fuel efficiency in the aviation industry, however, and the lower likelihood of tankering and the rapid anticipated growth in air transport, there are definite advantages to be gained from sub-global taxation (for example at EU level) of aviation bunker fuels.

Flexibility mechanisms and trade

The 'flexibility mechanisms' of the Kyoto Protocol – the emissions trading system, joint implementation, and the clean development mechanism – form together some of the most interesting aspects of the agreement. Since they are essentially trading mechanisms, an obvious question to ask is to what extent these are likely to be compatible with the MTS.

It seems unlikely that emissions reductions units would automatically be considered to be recognizable items under the WTO, though even if they were, and were therefore subject to WTO disciplines of openness and non-discrimination, this seems unlikely to cause any particular problem. It is more likely that the trading systems themselves – the infrastructure of brokers and exchanges – would be considered to be services under the General Agreement on Trade in Services. It is also probable that the initial allocation of permits may fall under the disciplines of the WTO Agreement on Subsidies and Countervailing Measures. In the final analysis, however, these questions will probably be settled by negotiation between the parties to both sets of treaties. The question that needs to be asked is therefore whether the involvement of the highly-evolved and effective WTO system in the new global emissions market to be created under the Kyoto Protocol could be actively helpful to the operation of the flexibility mechanisms of the Protocol; the answer is almost certainly affirmative.

Trade measures and the Kyoto Protocol

The non-compliance provisions of the climate change regime are still in their infancy. It is conceivable, however, that in due course they may benefit from the inclusion of trade measures (trade bans and/or other restrictive measures) such as those employed in the Montreal Protocol (alongside a range of other measures) in persuading non-parties to adhere to the regime and as a sanction against non-complying parties. This raises questions of technical feasibility and also of the inter-relationship with the MTS which can, however, be resolved.

The implementation of the Protocol may also lead to the development of trade restrictions between parties (as in the Montreal Protocol), including measures such as those described in Chapters 3 and 4, on energy efficiency standards, energy/carbon taxes and subsidies. Once again there are potential interactions with the MTS that need to be discussed and resolved.

Chapter 1

Introduction and background

This book is about one particular aspect of the interaction of two of the key driving forces of international relations in the modern world, trade liberalization and environmental protection. It deals with the relationship between international trade and policies designed to mitigate climate change.

Trade forms an increasingly important aspect of international relations. The volume of world trade in goods topped $5 trillion for the first time in 1996, having grown at an average rate of about 8 per cent a year since the signing of the Marrakesh agreement in 1994 marking the completion of the Uruguay Round of trade negotiations begun in 1986.[1] The multilateral trading system (MTS) overseen by the World Trade Organization (WTO) now covers areas such as agriculture, services, intellectual property, textiles, technical barriers to trade, and health standards, representing a significant extension in scope compared to its pre-Uruguay Round version; it is likely to be further developed in the proposed Millennium Round of trade negotiations scheduled to begin at the end of 1999. Since the scope of trade policy is so much wider than hitherto, in turn this means that trade regulation increasingly impinges on other areas of policy, such as environmental protection. As the chair of a WTO dispute panel described it, 'trade policy and regulation [now] emerge as the prime instruments of foreign policy. They take centre stage. Enforcement of foreign policies essentially operates with economic incentives, of which market access assumes a key role. Traditional means, such as territorial control or military operations, are no longer suitable and available'.[2]

---

[1] The rate of growth in world trade reached a peak of 10% in 1997, with the value of merchandise exports reaching $5.3 trillion, before falling to 3.5% in 1998, largely as a result of the drastic economic contraction in Asia and the collapse in oil prices.

[2] Thomas Cottier, 'The WTO and Environmental Law: Some Issues and Ideas', paper delivered at WTO Symposium on Trade, Environment and Sustainable Development, Geneva, 17–18 March 1998.

At the same time, climate change has emerged in recent years as the most serious of the many global environmental concerns. A complex political, scientific and public debate culminated in the negotiation of the 1997 Kyoto Protocol, incorporating a legally binding obligation on industrialized countries to reduce emissions of greenhouse gases on average by 5.2 per cent below 1990 levels by the period 2008–12. If implemented, the Kyoto Protocol is likely to be the most far-reaching multilateral environmental agreement (MEA) to have been agreed to date, with a marked impact in particular on the way in which modern economies generate and use energy. The successful tackling of the challenges posed by climate change – for which the Kyoto Protocol is only a first step – will imply a major shift in consumer attitudes and behaviour, technological innovation and investment decisions.

The purpose of this book is to explore the nature of the possible interactions between the requirements of the Kyoto Protocol, and policies and measures that are adopted in response to it, and international patterns of trade and their legal framework, the multilateral trading system. This chapter sets out the background, first to the climate change issue and then to the debate around trade and the environment.

1.1 Climate change and the Kyoto Protocol

The greenhouse effect is a natural part of the earth's climatic system. The presence in the atmosphere of 'greenhouse gases', including carbon dioxide, methane, volatile organic compounds, nitrous oxide, ozone and water vapour, traps a proportion of the solar radiation reaching the earth and raises the temperature of the surface well above the level it would otherwise be – indeed, without this process, surface temperature would be too low to support life as we know it. If the concentration of these gases is raised, however, it seems logical that the earth's surface temperature would increase in response – and since this in turn influences factors such as ocean currents, cloud formation and rainfall, climatic patterns could change quite dramatically. Since carbon dioxide is a byproduct of the burning of the fossil fuels – coal, oil and gas – on which modern economies depend so heavily, it seems quite possible that human activities can thereby directly affect climate.

As early as 1827, the French scientist Fourier postulated a link between atmospheric concentrations of carbon dioxide and increased temperature, and in 1908 the Swedish scientist Arrhenius published calculations predicting that a doubling in atmospheric carbon dioxide concentrations would raise global temperatures by approximately 4°C. Further scientific investigations tended to support this hypothesis and, in the wake of growing international concern over the state of the global environment in the 1970s and 1980s, the United Nations Environment Programme (UNEP) and the World Meteorological Organization (WMO) established the Intergovernmental Panel on Climate Change (IPCC) in 1988. The IPCC, incorporating the work of 2500 scientists from around the world, was charged with preparing the first international scientific assessment of the potential risks of 'global warming'.

The Panel's First Assessment Report was published in 1990. The science section of the report critically examined the body of evidence in support of the global warming hypothesis and reviewed the theoretical and empirical foundations of the various climate models. Its key conclusion was that rising concentrations of carbon dioxide and other greenhouse gases in the atmosphere were caused by human activities and would cause global temperatures to rise, with accompanying climatic changes. Its central estimate was a temperature increase of 0.3°C (±0.15°C) per decade, the fastest rate seen in the past 10,000 years. While the report studiously documented widespread uncertainties over the precise impacts of such temperature rises, it concluded that '... the potentially serious consequences of climate change on the global environment give sufficient reasons to begin adopting response strategies that can be justified immediately in the face of significant uncertainties ...'.[3]

The IPCC's Second Assessment Report was released in 1996. This second survey was markedly more decisive in tone than its predecessor. Its main scientific findings included the fact that greenhouse gas concentrations had continued to increase as a result of human activities: carbon dioxide (the most important greenhouse gas), for example,

---

[3] Intergovernmental Panel on Climate Change, *Climate Change: The Scientific Assessment* (Cambridge University Press, 1990).

had increased in atmospheric concentration by nearly 30 per cent from pre-industrial times, and methane concentrations had almost doubled. Global mean surface temperature had increased by 0.3–0.6°C since the late 19th century, and recent years had been among the warmest since at least 1860. Global sea level had risen by 10–25 cm over the past century and it was likely that much of this rise was temperature-related (due mainly to thermal expansion of the oceans); there had also been changes in extreme weather events (heavier rainfall, hurricanes, etc.) in certain regions, though their relationship to wider climatic change was still unclear. The report concluded that 'the observed warming trend was unlikely to be entirely natural in origin', and that 'the balance of evidence suggests a discernible human influence on global climate'.[4]

Other sections of the report found that significant 'no regrets' opportunities were available in most countries to reduce emissions of greenhouse gases at no net cost, and also that the potential risk of damage from climate change was enough to justify action beyond such no regrets measures. In the absence of any mitigating policy measures, global mean surface air temperature was projected to rise by about 2°C by the year 2100 (in addition to what may have been induced to date), with a range of uncertainty of 1–3.5°C. Even if stabilization of greenhouse gas concentrations were achieved, temperature would continue to increase beyond this point because of the thermal inertia of the oceans; assuming stabilization in 2100, only 50–90 per cent of the eventual temperature change would have occurred by then. Sea levels would rise, with a mid-range estimate of 50 cm by 2100 (range 15–95 cm), and would continue rising for centuries thereafter.

The publication of the reports, together with a growing environmental consciousness world-wide, and increasing awareness of oddities in weather patterns, helped ensure that climate change became as much a social, economic and political issue as it was a scientific one; it moved from the back pages of obscure academic journals to the front pages of national newspapers. This growing scientific and public pressure fed

---

[4] Intergovernmental Panel on Climate Change, *Climate Change 1995: The Science of Climate Change* (Cambridge University Press, 1996).

into the negotiation of the United Nations Framework Convention on Climate Change (FCCC), adopted during the United Nations Conference on Environment and Development (UNCED), the 'Earth Summit' held in Rio de Janeiro in June 1992.

The FCCC was the result of 15 months of negotiations. It set as its ultimate objective the 'stabilisation of greenhouse gas concentrations in the atmosphere at a level that would prevent dangerous anthropogenic interference with the earth's climate system'. Such a level should be achieved, stated the Convention, within a time frame sufficient to allow ecosystems to adapt naturally to climate change, to ensure that food production is not threatened, and to enable economic development to proceed in a sustainable manner. The Convention established the principle that climate change was a serious problem and action could not wait upon the resolution of scientific uncertainties. Developed countries were to take the lead, providing compensation for any additional costs undertaken by developing countries. Given strong opposition from the US, no binding policy commitments were included, but the FCCC indicated that industrialized countries (strictly speaking, Annex I countries, listed in the Convention[5]) should agree as a first step to return greenhouse gas emissions to 1990 levels by 2000 – a target which will not now be met by the US, Japan or a number of other OECD countries. The Convention entered into force in March 1994, and by June 1999 had been ratified by 179 countries.

In the years immediately following the signing of the agreement it became clear that a voluntary target alone would be insufficient to meet the Convention's stated objectives. By 1997 CO_2 emissions from the United States and Japan had grown by more than 10 per cent despite their commitments under the FCCC, and discounting the recent declines in the former Soviet Union, world-wide emissions had contin-

---

[5] FCCC Annex I Parties now include Australia, Austria, Belgium, Bulgaria, Canada, Croatia, the Czech Republic, Denmark, Estonia, Finland, France, Germany, Greece, Hungary, Iceland, Ireland, Italy, Japan, Latvia, Liechtenstein, Lithuania, Luxembourg, Monaco, The Netherlands, New Zealand, Norway, Poland, Portugal, Romania, the Russian Federation, Slovakia, Slovenia, Spain, Switzerland, Turkey, Ukraine, the United Kingdom and the United States.

ued to increase at more than 2 per cent per annum.[6] In March 1995 the
first Conference of the Parties to the FCCC met in Berlin to assess
progress towards the objectives of the Convention. The Conference
agreed that the voluntary commitments specified in Article 4.2 of the
Convention were insufficient to meet the intent of the agreement, and
that a specific legal instrument would be required to strengthen commitments beyond 2000. The Conference adopted the 'Berlin Mandate', setting out the principles guiding the development of a protocol
to set legally binding targets and timetables to reduce greenhouse gas
emissions. Developing countries succeeded in including within the
Berlin Mandate provisions that they be excluded from any such binding obligations. The Mandate formed the basis of the following two
and a half years of negotiations, culminating in the third Conference of
the Parties in Kyoto in December 1997.

The Kyoto Protocol[7]

The Kyoto Protocol to the United Nations Framework Convention on
Climate Change was formally adopted on 11 December 1997, after a
protracted and exhausting final negotiating session. When in force, the
Protocol will establish a legally binding obligation on Annex I countries to reduce emissions of greenhouse gases on average by 5.2 per
cent below 1990 levels by the period 2008–12. These 'quantified
emission limitation and reduction commitments' are differentiated between countries, and listed in Annex B to the Protocol. For the major
players, the EU's target is 8 per cent below 1990 levels, the US's 7 per
cent below and Japan's 6 per cent below. Relative to a business-as-
usual scenario, such commitments equate to real reductions in greenhouse gas emissions of approximately 20–40 per cent, to be achieved
within a 14-year period. The commitments listed in Annex B cover a
basket of the six principal anthropogenic greenhouse gases – carbon di-

[6] B. Bolin, 'The Kyoto Negotiations on Climate Change: A Science Perspective', *Science* 279 (1998).
[7] For a comprehensive analysis of the content and negotiation of the Kyoto Protocol, see Michael Grubb, with Christiaan Vrolijk and Duncan Brack, *The Kyoto Protocol: A Guide and Assessment* (London: RIIA/Earthscan, 1999).

oxide, methane, nitrous oxide, hydrofluorocarbons, perfluorocarbons and sulphur hexafluoride – and take into account emissions arising from changes in forest and land use patterns.

Commitments are to achieved in a number of ways. Article 2 of the Protocol commits each Annex I party to 'implement and/or further elaborate policies and measures in accordance with its national circumstances', and then lists a wide range of potential areas for action, including energy efficiency enhancement, the use of renewable energy sources and the removal of market imperfections, such as subsidies, running counter to the objectives of the FCCC. Cooperation with other parties is called for in order to enhance the effectiveness of national policies. Parties are to work through the International Civil Aviation Organization and the International Maritime Organization to reduce greenhouse gas emissions from aviation and maritime travel.

In addition to this framework of domestic measures, however, the Protocol also contains a series of 'flexibility mechanisms' (later and less contentiously called 'Kyoto mechanisms') designed to reduce emissions through international cooperation. These include international emissions trading (Article 17), the clean development mechanism (Article 12) and joint implementation (Article 6), all of which are intended to optimize the cost-effectiveness of emissions reduction initiatives and lower the cost of complying with the respective emission targets assumed under the Protocol. Together they have the potential to create an international market for greenhouse gas (and particularly carbon) abatement, with profound implications for the international economy.

As with the FCCC, developing countries are not subject to any commitments, though the clean development mechanism provides a route through which emissions reduction initiatives in their countries can contribute to achieving the overall targets. Parties not included in Annex I can volunteer to adopt their own targets, however, and during 1998 two developing countries – Argentina and Kazakhstan – announced their intention to do just that.

Several issues were left unresolved at Kyoto, including most of the details of the flexibility mechanisms and any non-compliance system. These are to be settled by succeeding conferences of the parties to the

FCCC (which will act as meetings of the parties to the Protocol, when that enters into force). After a distinct lack of progress in negotiations leading up the fourth Conference of the Parties, in Buenos Aires in November 1998, the Conference resolved to adopt the 'Buenos Aires Plan of Action' setting out timetables for decision-making on particular aspects. As of July 1999, 84 countries had signed the Protocol and 12 had ratified it. It will enter into force when 55 parties, including Annex I parties accounting for at least 55 per cent of the Annex I carbon dioxide emissions in 1990, have ratified it.

1.2 The trade and environment debate

Climate change is the latest, and probably the most significant, of the global environmental concerns that form the background to the debate around the inter-relationship of international trade and environmental protection. The international community is in theory committed *both* to trade liberalisation, through the establishment of the WTO at the conclusion of the Uruguay Round in 1995, and to environmentally sustainable development, through Agenda 21, the blueprint for sustainable development unanimously adopted at UNCED in 1992. Indeed, the latter states that: 'an open, multilateral trading system, supported by the adoption of sound environmental policies would have a positive impact on the environment and contribute to sustainable development'.[8]

Trade, investment and the environment

In many instances trade liberalization can indeed contribute to sustainable development. According to the theory of comparative advantage, trade allows countries to specialize in the production of goods and services in which they are relatively most efficient – in other words, to maximize output from a given input of resources, which is a movement in the direction of environmental sustainability. Furthermore,

---

[8] United Nations Conference on Environment and Development, Agenda 21, Chapter 2, Section B.

trade liberalization can help to remove distortionary subsidies and pricing policies that sustain environmentally harmful activities and encourage the spread of environmentally friendly technology. The higher rate of growth of income resulting from trade also helps to generate the resource needed for investment in environmental protection – although this is not an automatic link, and, as was observed in Agenda 21, appropriate environmental policies need to be pursued simultaneously.

Trade can also, however, harm the environment. As well as the composition and technology effects of trade liberalization – the changes in production and techniques referred to above – there is also the scale effect, the expansion of production and consumption as markets develop and income grows. Taken in isolation, this is likely to prove damaging to the environment, particularly since in modern economies the costs and benefits of environmental externalities are generally not incorporated in prices and decision-taking. As economies expand, therefore, they tend to increase both their output of pollution and their consumption of non-renewable resources.

The development of environmental regulation can, of course, offset this, and reductions in recent years in the output of sulphur dioxide (which causes acid deposition or 'acid rain') and in ozone-depleting substances, such as chlorofluorocarbons (CFCs), at least in industrialized countries, are a tribute to their efficacy. However, increasing environmental standards raise the issue of international competitiveness. It is a common perception that higher environmental standards cause business costs to increase, reducing profits and possibly inducing migration, of investment flows if not of industrial plant itself, to countries with less stringent regulatory regimes, where the cost of production is lower. In fact this is a complex area with a dearth of empirical evidence.[9] Most research indicates that environmental standards play no significant part in investment location decisions, largely because the costs associated with them are relatively low; many other matters, in-

---

[9] See Lyuba Zarsky, 'Havens, Halos and Spaghetti: Untangling the Evidence about FDI and the Environment' (paper for OECD conference on FDI and the Environment, January 1999), for a good summary.

cluding political stability, potential of domestic markets, quality of infrastructure, labour costs and ease of repatriation of profits are of greater importance in governing a firm's investment decisions. A recent study of Japanese companies concluded that although they complain about high production costs at home, this seldom drives them actually to invest overseas. Meeting overseas demand or following competitors to new markets were found to be much more decisive factors in directing investment to other countries.[10]

While true in general, however, some specific industry sectors may be more drastically affected by environmental policy. In particular, the successful implementation of the Kyoto Protocol, not to mention any further evolution in its greenhouse gas reduction commitments, is almost bound to require increases in the cost of carbon-intensive energy sources. This will have a major impact on energy-intensive industries such as the iron and steel, or aluminium, industries, where energy consumption may account for up to 15–20 per cent of total costs. Furthermore, as with any measure where the benefits are diffuse and widespread but the costs are concentrated, political lobbies *against* action may often prove stronger than lobbies *for*. Political decision-makers often tend to behave as though they believe that environmental regulation does invariably raise costs. Thus competitiveness concerns are likely to remain an important part of the debate.

The multilateral trading system

The other main area of interaction between trade and environmental policies arises from the potential for conflict between the legal regimes which govern them. Environmental policy invariably develops at different speeds in different countries. Trade rules, set internationally, may fail to allow for such differences in national efforts at achieving environmental sustainability, even when policies are aimed at controlling transboundary or global environmental problems. In addition, a number of important multilateral environmental agreements (MEAs)

---

[10] S. Dasgupta, S. Moody, and S. Sinha, *Japanese Multinationals in Asia: Capabilities and Motivations* (Washington, DC: World Bank, 1995).

require parties to apply trade restrictions as means of achieving their objectives. All this may lead to conflict with the multilateral trading system centred around the General Agreement on Tariffs and Trade and overseen by the WTO.

The central aim of the multilateral trading system is to liberalize trade between WTO members. Its core principles are to be found in the following articles of the GATT:

- GATT Articles I ('most favoured nation' treatment) and III ('national treatment') outlaw discrimination in trade: WTO members are not permitted to discriminate between traded 'like products' produced by other WTO members, or between domestic and international like products.
- GATT Article XI ('elimination of quantitative restrictions') forbids any restrictions other than duties, taxes or other charges on imports from and exports to other WTO members.
- GATT Article III requires imported and domestic like products to be treated identically with respect to internal taxes and regulations.

WTO members, in other words, are not permitted to discriminate between other WTO members' traded products, or between domestic and international production. Successive GATT trade rounds have both reduced tariff and non-tariff barriers to trade and extended these principles to ever-wider ranges of traded goods and services – and so essentially the same principles are built into all the other WTO agreements which have developed alongside the GATT.

The GATT does, however, permit certain unilateral trade restrictions for various reasons, including the pursuit of environmental protection under particular circumstances. Article XX ('General Exceptions') states that:

> Subject to the requirement that such measures are not applied in a manner which would constitute a means of arbitrary or unjustifiable discrimination between countries where the same conditions prevail, or a disguised restriction on international trade, nothing in this Agreement shall be construed to prevent the adoption or enforcement by any contracting party of measures:

... (b) necessary to protect human, animal or plant life or health;

... (g) relating to the conservation of exhaustible natural resources if such measures are made effective in conjunction with restrictions on domestic production or consumption.

So although the GATT in general frowns on trade restrictions, countries can ban or restrict the import of products which will harm their own environments – as long as the standards applied are non-discriminatory between countries and between domestic and foreign production. As the GATT Secretariat expressed it in 1992 '... GATT rules place essentially no constraints on a country's right to protect its own environment against damage from either domestic production or the consumption of domestically produced or imported products ...'.[11]

Various Uruguay Round agreements, including the Agreement on Technical Barriers to Trade (TBT Agreement), and the Agreement on the Application of Sanitary and Phytosanitary Measures (SPS Agreement), govern the application of potentially trade-restrictive measures in the fields of health and technical standards. The TBT Agreement, for example, aims to encourage international harmonization of product standards and to avoid their use as disguised protectionism. Under paragraph 2.2 of the Agreement, technical regulations shall not be more trade-restrictive than necessary to fulfil a 'legitimate objective' – defined as including environmental protection. Environmental grounds have indeed become more widely cited as an objective and rationale for applying trade-restrictive regulations including, most notably, measures aimed at controlling air pollution and hazardous chemicals.[12]

The WTO itself contains a reference to sustainable development in the preamble of the agreement establishing the body: 'The Parties to this Agreement, recognising that their relations in the field of trade and economic endeavour should be conducted with a view to raising standards of living ... and expanding the production of and trade in goods and services, while allowing for the optimal use of the world's resources in accordance with the objective of sustainable development,

[11] *International Trade 1990–91* (Geneva: GATT Secretariat, 1992) p. 23.
[12] Ibid., p. 32.

seeking both to protect and preserve the environment ...'. Initially regarded as little more than a symbolic acknowledgment of the issue, it
has been treated with considerably more significance since the WTO
Appellate Body cited it as an acceptable justification for particular
trade measures in the 1998 shrimp-turtle dispute, where the US imposed an embargo on imports of shrimp caught in nets not fitted with
turtle excluder devices, which prevent the incidental deaths of large
numbers of endangered species of sea turtles.[13]

It would appear, therefore, that the multilateral trading system poses
no threat to environmental regulation as long as environmental laws
and policies are applied in a non-discriminatory manner. In fact, however, there are two cases in which there *might* be a strong environmental justification for behaving differently: where processes, rather than
products, cause the environmental damage; and in the enforcement of
MEAs.

Process and production methods

The problem with trade restrictions based on environmental regulations derived from process and production *methods* (PPMs), as opposed to *product* standards, stems from the meaning of the GATT term
'like product'. This has become one of the most difficult issues in the
trade-environment arena. Originally incorporated into the GATT in order to prevent discrimination on the grounds of national origin, GATT
and WTO dispute panels have in general interpreted the term more
broadly to prevent discrimination in cases where *process* methods,
rather than *product* characteristics, have been the distinguishing char-
acteristic of the product and the justification for trade measures. In the
well-known US–Mexico tuna-dolphin dispute in 1991, for example,

---

[13] 'While Article XX was not modified in the Uruguay Round, the preamble attached to the
WTO Agreement shows that the signatories to that Agreement were, in 1994, fully aware of
the importance and legitimacy of environmental protection as a goal of national and
international policy...' (WTO: United States – Import Prohibition of Certain Shrimp and
Shrimp Products, Report of the Appellate Body, 12 October 1998 (WT/D558/A8/R), para.
129). This line of argument has potentially very wide implications, which is probably why it
generated almost as much criticism from the complainants in the case as from the defendant.

the dispute panel ruled that the trade restriction in question (the US import ban on Mexican tuna caught with dolphin-unfriendly nets) was in breach of the GATT because it discriminated against a product on the basis of the way in which it was produced, not on the basis of its own characteristics – i.e. it discriminated against a 'like product'.

In 1994, another GATT panel, ruling on an EU–US dispute over car imports, slightly relaxed the definition, considering that vehicles of different fuel efficiency standards could be considered *not* to be like products. However, it placed strict boundaries on this conclusion, arguing that Article III of the GATT referred only to a 'product as a product, from its introduction into the market to its final consumption'.[14] Factors relating to the manufacture of the product before its introduction into the market were, therefore, still irrelevant. Another panel in 1996 found that chemically-identical imported and domestic gasoline were like products, regardless of the environmental standards of the producers.

It is worth noting, however, that the term 'like product' is nowhere defined in the GATT, and in other areas the distinction between products and PPMs is not maintained. Both the Agreement on Subsidies and Countervailing Measures and the Agreement on Trade-Related Aspects of Intellectual Property Rights (the TRIPS Agreement) regulate some aspects of *how* goods are produced, allowing importing countries to discriminate against products if they are produced using excessive subsidy or misappropriated intellectual property. GATT's Article XX(e) allows countries to discriminate against products produced using prison labour. In addition, the GATT Secretariat's first (1971) report on trade and environment stated that a 'shared resource, such as a lake or the atmosphere, which is being polluted by foreign producers may give rise to restrictions on trade in the product of that process justifiable on grounds of the public interest in the importing country of control over a process carried out in an adjacent or nearby country.[15]

Furthermore, there are some signs that the WTO's Appellate Body may be modifying its approach in more recent disputes. In both the

---

[14] GATT: US: Taxes on Automobiles (1994): Report of the Panel, (DS 31/R) para. 5.52.
[15] Quoted in Steve Charnovitz, 'GATT and the environment: examining the issues', *International Environmental Affairs* 4:3, Summer 1992, p. 204.

reformulated gasoline case of 1996 and the shrimp-turtle dispute of 1998, the Appellate Body overturned the original dispute panels' arguments in some important respects (though upholding their conclusions, which were in each case to find against the restrictions on trade imposed by the US). The Appellate Body's main objection to the measures employed in the two cases appeared to be to the *way* in which they were applied – which was found to be 'arbitrary and unjustifiably discriminatory' in the terms of the headnote to Article XX – rather than the basis on which they rested. Although it was not stated explicitly, the implication could be that PPM-based trade restrictions which were applied in a fashion which did not discriminate in any way other than on the basis of the means of production of the goods in question, might be acceptable.

This is, however, a complex debate. Where the pollution caused by the PPM is confined to the locality of the process, PPM-based environmental trade measures are not easy to justify. Different parts of the world vary widely in their ability to assimilate pollution, depending on factors such as climate, population density, existing levels of pollution and risk preferences. Environmental regulations suited to industrialized nations, with high population densities and environments which have been subject to pollution for the past 200 years, may be wholly inappropriate for newly industrializing countries with much lower population densities and inherited pollution levels – and yet trade measures based on PPMs could in effect seek to impose the higher standards regardless. Carried to its logical extreme, enforcing similarity of PPMs could deny the very basis of comparative advantage, which rests on the proposition that countries possess different cost structures for the production of various goods. It is hardly surprising that many developing countries view the motives of those wishing to introduce the PPM issue to the debate as protectionist – what Deepak Lal, in an allusion to Kipling, called '... a green variant of the 19th century's "white man's burden"'.[16]

Where the pollution is transboundary or global, however, the argument is different, since the impact of the PPM is not confined to the

---

[16] D. Lal, 'Trade Blocs and Multilateral Free Trade', *Journal of Common Market Studies* 31 (1993), pp. 356–7.

country of origin. PPM-based measures are, furthermore, becoming increasingly important in strategies for environmental sustainability. Particularly where the use of energy is involved (as it is in virtually every manufacturing and processing activity), the pollution caused stems from the process and not the product. Life-cycle approaches, and ecolabelling schemes based on them, have similarly focused attention on the way in which products are manufactured, grown, or harvested as well on product characteristics themselves; indeed, the whole point of ecolabelling schemes is to provide information on differences in characteristics between like products.

Inclusion of PPM-based trade measures in MEAs may provide a solution, and in fact the Montreal Protocol (on ozone-depleting substances) includes provision for such measures, though they have not so far been deployed. GATT and WTO panels have repeatedly stressed the desirability of multilateral rather than unilateral action; part of the original panel's argument against the US action in the shrimp-turtle case was that the US had not attempted to enter into negotiations on a potential multilateral agreement before it imposed the import ban. The negotiation of international treaties is frequently, however, a difficult and slow process – as the failure, in February 1999, to agree the text of the draft Biosafety Protocol (aimed to control trade in genetically modified organisms) demonstrates. A number of participants in the debate[17] have therefore called for the GATT to be amended to set out objective criteria under which trade measures directed against PPMs could be taken (including requirements such as non-discriminatory and transparent measures and evidence of significant transboundary environmental problems), subject to challenge under normal GATT rules. In effect, this represents a redefinition of the term 'like product' in the context of a world in which environmental policy requiring the control of PPMs may justify trade policies which are not protectionist in intent but may look so when viewed from the perspective in which

---

[17] See in particular Paul Ekins, *Harnessing Trade to Sustainable Development* (Oxford: Green College, 1995), pp. 10–11; and Natural Resources Defense Council/Foundation for International Environmental Law and Development, *Environmental Priorities for the World Trading System* (Washington, DC: NRDC, 1995), p. 9.

the GATT was written 50 years ago.[18] As noted above, this may be the direction in which the WTO Appellate Body is itself beginning to move.

Multilateral environmental agreements

The other case in which there may be a strong environmental justification for the discriminatory application of trade restrictions is where these are required under the terms of a multilateral environmental agreement.

As Principle 12 of the Rio Declaration states, international agreement is clearly preferable to unilateral action in tackling transboundary or global environmental problems. Almost 200 MEAs already exist, of which about 20 incorporate trade measures. These include three of the most important: the Basel Convention on hazardous waste, the Convention on International Trade in Endangered Species (CITES), and the Montreal Protocol on ozone-depleting substances. In the absence of any comprehensive framework of global environmental law, the negotiation of further MEAs will form an increasingly prominent part of the international agenda.

Trade restrictions required by MEAs have been designed to realize four major objectives:

1. To restrict markets for environmentally hazardous products or goods produced unsustainably.
2. To increase the coverage of the agreement's provisions by encouraging governments to join and/or comply with the MEA.
3. To prevent free-riding (where non-participants enjoy the advantages of the MEA without incurring its costs) by encouraging governments to join and/or comply with the MEA.

---

[18] As Thomas Cottier has argued, the 'approach of construing the term like product in accordance with the very purpose of GATT and therefore in terms of prohibiting protectionist aims or effects of product differentiation is more suitable not only to the role of panels, but also leaves governments the necessary scope to pursue legitimate trade-related policies'. (Cottier, 'The WTO and Environmental Law', p. 5).

4. To ensure the MEA's effectiveness by preventing leakage – the situation where non-participants increase their emissions, or other unsustainable behaviour, as a result of the control measures taken by signatories.

Effectively, therefore, these MEAs restrict trade either because the trade itself is causing the environmental damage, and/or as an enforcement measure, to ensure that the agreement's objectives are not undermined by non-participation. The Montreal Protocol, for example, requires parties to ban imports of CFCs and other controlled substances from non-parties. On the face of it, this would appear to conflict with the GATT, since it discriminates between the same product imported from different countries on the basis of their membership of the Protocol. It is widely accepted, however, that the inclusion of this measure in the Montreal Protocol has contributed significantly to its success in attracting signatories.[19]

This topic has become one of the main items of debate within the trade-environment agenda in recent years, and was a particularly important topic in discussions in the WTO's Committee on Trade and Environment[20] in its first two years of existence, during the run-up to the Singapore WTO conference in 1996. Members put forward proposals designed variously to define under what conditions trade measures taken pursuant to an MEA could be considered to be 'necessary' under the terms of GATT's Article XX, or to establish a degree of WTO oversight on the negotiation and operation of trade provisions in future MEAs.[21] The EU pressed for an amendment to the GATT itself to create a presumption of compatibility with MEAs, but no consensus was

---

[19] See Duncan Brack, *International Trade and the Montreal Protocol* (London: RIIA/ Earthscan, 1996), for a full discussion.

[20] Established on the formation of the WTO, to 'identify the relationship between trade measures and environmental measures, in order to promote sustainable development [and] to make appropriate recommendations on whether any modifications of the provisions of the multilateral trading system are required ....' – WTO: Trade and Environment Decision, 14 April 1994.

[21] See Duncan Brack, 'Reconciling the GATT and Multilateral Environmental Agreements with Trade Provisions: The Latest Debate', *Review of European Community and International Environmental Law* 6:2, July 1997.

reached about the need for modifications to trade rules. The CTE noted, however, that:

> Trade measures based on specifically agreed-upon provisions can also be needed in certain cases to achieve the environmental objectives of an MEA, particularly where trade is related directly to the source of an environmental problem. They have played an important role in some MEAs in the past, and they may be needed to play a similarly important role in certain cases in the future.[22]

It is worth noting, however, that no complaint has yet arisen within the GATT or WTO with respect to trade measures taken in pursuit of an MEA, and this may continue to be the case; in instances such as the Montreal Protocol, where the trade provisions were designed to encourage countries to accede, this has been so successful that there are virtually no non-parties left against whom trade measures could be taken in any case. On the other hand, it is quite likely that future MEAs – such as the convention on persistent organic pollutants, or possibly the Kyoto Protocol – may benefit from the inclusion of trade restrictions. It is obviously desirable that negotiators are not inhibited from discussing them by the fear of a potential GATT challenge, and in a number of instances (including the Biosafety Protocol) countries opposed to the aims of the MEA in question have attempted to do just that.

Trade and environment: resolving the debate

The trade and environment debate is not going to go away. On the contrary, the combination of the steady growth in trade and the accumulating evidence of global environmental degradation, together with the pressure for international action that results, seems likely to lead to more, and more serious, conflicts. The very first dispute to be resolved under the new WTO was on a trade-environment case (the Reformulated Gasoline dispute), and there have been a number since.

---

[22] Report (1996) of the Committee on Trade and Environment, para 173.

The WTO's Committee on Trade and Environment seems unlikely to resolve the potential conflict. Despite prolonged discussions in its first two years of its existence, the CTE's first report, in 1997, was able to conclude little more than that further work was needed, and in its deliberations since it has not generally attempted to reach consensus. One major problem is that most participants in the CTE, particularly those from developing countries, are drawn from a trade background and perspective, and trade liberalization is in general a more important objective for most governments than environmental protection. The shared values, assumptions and operating modes of such a group provide a powerful underlying momentum in the direction of further trade liberalization, and against any measure which is seen as running counter to this trend, whether or not it is properly understood. The environmental argument is thus weakened before it is even put forward – though more recent discussions in the CTE, freed from the pressures of having to agree anything, do seem to have proved somewhat more educational than hitherto.

A more fruitful way forward may be the inclusion of particular proposals – such as a GATT amendment or WTO agreement on MEAs, as one element of a package of measures of benefit to the causes of trade liberalization and development as well as environment (such as, for example, the further liberalization of trade in agriculture) – adopted as part of a future trade round. At the time of writing, it does seem more likely than not that 'trade and environment' will feature in some form as a component of the forthcoming Millennium Round. What is still needed however, is detailed preparation and analytical work on what aspects of the very wide trade and environment debate can be most usefully carried forward. This book aims to make a contribution to that debate with reference to the issue of climate change.

1.3 International trade and climate change policies

The rest of the book deals with the interaction of climate change policies with trade policies and with trade patterns. There are three broad areas of likely interaction:

1. Policies adopted to mitigate climate change may lead to changes in international competitiveness and in aggregate trade flows between countries: some may become net losers, and others net gainers. Alternatively, or additionally, these competitiveness impacts – real or perceived – may constrain policy choices.
2. Particular policies adopted in certain areas may create new trade barriers and/or open up new market opportunities.
3. The requirements of the multilateral trading system may constrain the adoption of particular climate change mitigation policies and/or particular aspects of the climate change regime; conversely, the development and effective implementation of the Kyoto Protocol might raise questions about the need to modify the WTO agreements.

In general, these issues are all of especial concern to developing countries, the group which has tended to argue most strongly in the WTO Committee on Trade and Environment against modifications to the MTS for environmental purposes. Although their arguments have often seemed exaggerated and unjustified, their position is entirely understandable given the slow progress made by industrialized countries in dismantling protectionist trade barriers which discriminate against developing country exports, such as in the areas of textiles and agriculture – and also the arguments put forward by some in the industrialized world for using trade barriers to enforce compliance with labour standards, human rights or animal welfare.

The fear that thinly-disguised protectionism is the underlying aim behind environmental justifications for new trade barriers is a real one, and led in part to the inclusion in Article 3 of the FCCC (which lists general principles) of the following paragraph:

> 3.5 The Parties should cooperate to promote a supportive and open international economic system that would lead to sustainable economic growth and development in all Parties, particularly developing country Parties, thus enabling them better to address the problems of climate change. Measures taken to combat climate change, including unilateral ones, should not constitute a means of arbitrary or unjustifiable discrimination or a disguised restriction on international trade.

The last sentence in particular is language taken almost straight from the GATT. Similarly, paragraph 3 of Article 2 of the Kyoto Protocol states the principle of protection of countries from any adverse effects of any of the policies and measures that may be adopted, including any adverse effects on international trade. It refers to Articles 4.8 and 4.9 of the FCCC, which list categories of developing countries particularly at risk – including obvious ones such as small island countries, or those with areas prone to natural disasters, but also including 'countries whose economies are highly dependent on income generated from the production, processing and export, and/or consumption of fossil fuels and associated energy-intensive products'.

What none of these agreements do, of course, is to lay down any principles to follow where the pursuit of some objectives (such as, for example, the promotion of energy efficiency) conflicts with that of others (for example, avoiding a reduction in fossil fuel imports). And although protectionist motivations may have underlain some of the trade restrictions countries have adopted, ostensibly for environmental purposes, so far the challenges posed by climate change are real and significant and will require major economic restructuring if they are to be met successfully. It is this potential clash between the objectives of climate change mitigation and trade liberalization which is the subject of the next six chapters.

Chapter 2 deals with the broad area of competitiveness and trade impacts of climate change mitigation measures, looking particularly at the effects on energy markets. Chapters 3 and 4 look at the interaction with trade and the MTS of two specific types of policies and measures that seem likely to be adopted (and in many cases are already being adopted) to reduce emissions of carbon dioxide: the greater use of minimum standards of efficiency of energy consumption for traded products (Chapter 3), and the application of energy or carbon taxes (Chapter 4). The area of environmental tax reform is touched on again in Chapter 5, which examines the taxation of international 'bunker fuels' (aviation and marine fuel), which are currently exempt from any taxation at all. Chapter 6 looks at the interaction between the MTS and the 'flexibility mechanisms' introduced in the Kyoto Protocol – emissions trading, and the clean development mechanism. Chapter 7 deals with the relationship between the Kyoto Protocol and the MTS, including in particular the potential role that trade measures may have to play in its enforcement.

Chapter 2

Trade impacts of climate change policies

This chapter deals with the potential overall impact on patterns of international trade of industrialized country actions to limit emissions of greenhouse gases, chiefly carbon dioxide.

The economic issues are complex, because they involve a balance between several different effects:

- Measures to limit emissions will reduce demand for fossil fuels: certainly for coal and probably for oil (the impact on gas is more uncertain and could be positive). This will tend to reduce both the overall volume of fossil fuel exports and their price. For reasons discussed below, this issue particularly concerns developing country oil exporters.

- If industrialized countries take measures that raise the costs of their manufactured goods, particularly energy- (or carbon-) intensive products, this will reduce the price-competitiveness of such goods and tend to lead to an increase in imports from countries (for example, developing countries) without such measures. Set against this, it will also raise the price of developing-country imports of manufactured products. Measures to exempt industry, or energy-intensive sectors, or to adjust taxes at the border would reduce or neutralize such effects (see further in Chapter 4).

- If industrialized country measures to reduce emissions affect overall levels of consumption and demand in industrialized countries, total import volumes are likely to fall. 'No-regrets' measures which both reduce emissions and improve economic performance, such as removing subsidies for fossil fuels or liberalizing energy markets, will tend to have a positive impact on the balance of trade with other countries, whilst more costly measures could reduce imports and change their composition, potentially (though not necessarily) with negative impacts.

- Climate change itself will affect levels of consumption, investment and trade – for example, through impacts on agriculture or the costs of storm damage. Abatement efforts will reduce these impacts.

This chapter discusses each of these issues, and then focuses more closely upon the implications for energy resources and markets, and the possible options for addressing the concerns of energy exporting countries – a category specifically mentioned in the Climate Change Convention (see section 1.3). The chapter also discusses the question of the 'leakage' of emissions from industrialized countries – i.e. the possibility that abatement within industrialized countries will have the effect of increasing emissions elsewhere, as industrial activity and investment migrate to avoid compliance costs, and the countervailing impact of emissions abatement in reducing over time the carbon intensity of the technologies and industrial practices that are involved in international trade.

2.1 Impacts on energy markets

Measures to reduce emissions of carbon dioxide will clearly affect energy markets, but the precise impact will depend upon the sectors at which the particular policies are directed. In most industrialized countries, the transport sector accounts for the bulk of oil consumption, whilst electricity and heating tend to be based more upon coal and natural gas. Experience to date suggests that countries have found easier and less costly means to reduce CO_2 emissions from electricity and heating, which is therefore likely to lead to a major impact upon coal. However, significant amounts of fuel oil are still used for power generation and heat supply, and this, combined with measures directed at transport, means that oil consumption is also likely to decline (relative to business as usual).

The main international trade impact is likely to lead from these effects on oil consumption. Although international coal trade is growing, most coal is still produced and consumed domestically and the aggregate value of coal exports from developing countries is a fraction of that of oil exports. In addition, the international traded price for coal is

**Figure 2.1: Energy export dependency and per capita GDP
(for countries with energy exports exceeding $2 bn)**

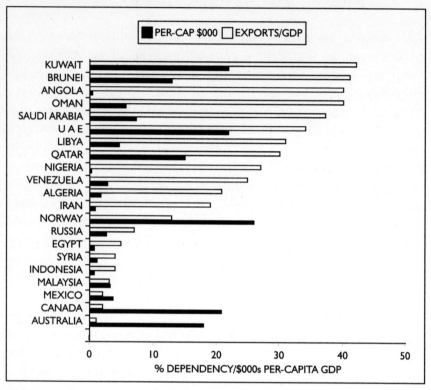

Source: Peter Kassler and Matthew Paterson, *Energy Exporters and Climate Change* (London: RIIA, 1997).

far closer to its production cost than is the case for oil; thus profits are less. Finally, coal resources are much less concentrated, and for no country do coal export revenues dominate total export earnings in the way that oil exports do for some countries (Figure 2.1). Figure 2.1 also shows that energy exporting countries vary greatly in their vulnerability to such effects; significant exporters range from very high to very low in their per-capita GDP, and similarly vary in their degree of dependence on energy exports.

A 1993 study by the Organization of Petroleum Exporting Countries (OPEC) projected that oil demand in 2010 would grow to about 78 million barrels per day (mb/d) in the absence of emission constraints, and that the carbon taxes proposed in the early 1990s (in the EC and US) would reduce global oil demand by 2.4mb/d to 75.4mb/d.[1] This in turn would reduce OPEC revenue to about $3900 billion from $4073 billion. A 10 per cent reduction in CO_2 emissions by 2010 relative to 1990 levels was estimated to reduce oil demand by 12.2mb/d and OPEC revenues by over $800 billion, giving a reduction in average GNP growth rates in OPEC countries from 3.87 per cent per year to 3.49 per cent. The OPEC study assumed high baseline growth, rising oil prices, and a relatively large impact of abatement on oil consumption (though this still grew in absolute terms in all cases), resulting in part from reduced global economic activity. For reasons discussed below, the impacts are likely to be smaller than this suggests. In fact, of course, the study's assumption of rising oil prices was very wide of the mark – the price per barrel collapsed from roughly $20 in 1993 to below $10 at the end of 1998, before beginning to turn up again, with a much greater impact on OPEC revenues than anticipated climate change policies.

Furthermore, the study assumed that abatement did not affect the oil price. Unless exporting countries successfully coordinate a price-raising response, which is unlikely, global oil prices would be expected to decline with reduced global demand. While increasing revenue losses to oil exporters, this would benefit the great majority of developing countries that are oil importers. One of the major impacts of industrialized country action on climate change may thus be to transfer revenue from oil exporters to importers (as compared with business-as-usual growth), and this may form one of the major political tensions arising from CO_2 constraints.

2.2 Impacts on energy-intensive goods

The manufacturing of traded products through relatively energy-intensive processes accounts for 10–20 per cent of CO_2 emissions in most industrialized countries. If CO_2 abatement in these countries raises the

---

[1] *The Impact of Environmental Measures on OPEC*, OPEC Energy Studies Department, Vienna, October 1993.

price of energy and hence production costs for these sectors, this represents a potential economic advantage for countries without such policies. Set against this, less industrialized developing countries that import manufactured goods from the industrialized world could face increased import bills. Various modelling studies discussed below highlight gains in trade in energy-intensive products for non-Annex I countries, particularly for countries like Korea and some Southeast Asian economies that already have a strong manufacturing base but are exempt from CO_2 controls (while other countries lose slightly). Some models suggest that this would be the dominant economic effect for these countries, which would gain both from lower oil prices and from more competitive exports.

So far, however, countries that have taken or seriously proposed action to limit CO_2 emissions have generally avoided measures that would seriously impact energy-intensive manufacturing; those countries that have imposed carbon taxes have generally exempted these sectors or at least adjusted tax rates at the border (see Chapter 4). In most countries, policy in the most energy-intensive sectors has not gone beyond voluntary agreements with the major companies involved. The total exemption of energy-intensive sectors would of course neutralize any potential economic costs and benefits for other countries, but would also limit the scope and efficiency of CO_2 controls, and place a heavier burden on non-energy intensive sectors. Rebating energy or carbon taxes for exports at the border, and imposing them on imports, would neutralize the competitiveness impacts of such taxes, but could be complex to administer and would probably be subject to challenge under the WTO agreements (see section 4.4).

Controlling emissions from energy-intensive sectors using systems of tradable emission permits rather than taxes would tend to reduce the competitiveness impacts (though it might affect investment decisions for new plant) and is perhaps the most likely approach for those industrialized countries that do move beyond complete exemptions. In general however, industrialized countries seem likely to implement policies in ways which do not seriously undermine competitiveness in these sectors, avoiding stronger action unless and until more coordinated international approaches can be developed. By the same token, the corresponding effects on trade in energy-intensive goods are likely to be modest.

2.3 Impacts of abatement on overall trade structure and volumes

If measures taken to limit CO_2 emissions have a significant impact on the overall level of consumption and demand in industrialized countries, total import volumes are likely to fall. The overall impact is complex and could be highly country-specific; it is also quite hard to predict, because CO_2 constraints could tend to change industrial structures and induce innovation in various ways, for example by stimulating the growth of new, lower-CO_2-emitting industries which might or might not involve increasing imports from other countries.

For the level of commitments agreed in the Kyoto Protocol, however, debate continues as to the overall economic impact within industrialized countries. 'No-regrets' measures which both reduce emissions and improve economic performance, such as removing subsidies for fossil fuels, liberalizing energy markets, or certain energy efficiency programmes, could contribute much of the emission reductions needed to attain the modest CO_2 reductions in industrialized countries required by the Protocol. Such measures will tend to have a positive impact on non-energy trade with other countries. The impact would also depend upon the specific nature and rate at which policies are imposed. Instruments such as emission trading across Annex 1 countries, by reducing the cost to industrialized countries, will also reduce the impacts on other countries. The scale of income-related trade effects is therefore highly debatable and dependent upon implementation mechanisms.

Furthermore, action in industrialized countries will have price as well as volume impacts. If emissions reduction policies change the relative prices of various products, this could increase imports not only of energy-intensive manufactured goods (from countries without similar policies), but also of energy-efficient products and low-carbon products such as renewable energy technologies (as domestic demand increases).[2] These

---

[2] N. Mabey, S. Hall, C. Smith and S. Gupta, *Argument in the Greenhouse: The International Economics of Climate Change* (London: Routledge, 1997); T. Forsyth, ed.,

Figure 2.2: Impacts on trade in non-Annex I exports for different trade price elasticities, 1997–2010

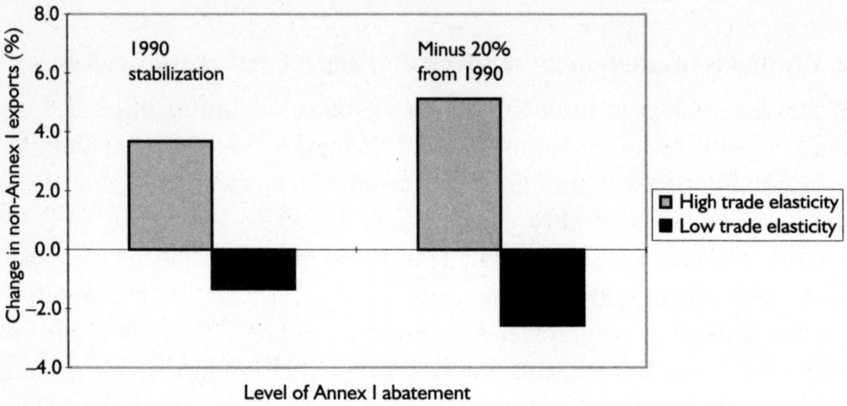

Source: N. Mabey, S. Hall, C. Smith and S. Gupta, *Argument in the Greenhouse: The International Economics of Climate Change* (London: Routledge, 1997).

positive price effects will become more important as the responsiveness of international trade to price differentials – the 'trade elasticity' – increases; Figure 2.2 shows that doubling the trade elasticity (including some relocation in energy-intensive sectors) would imply that the price effects of emissions constraints on trade would then outweigh the volume effects, leading to a net increase in trade volumes.

2.4 Effects of reduced climatic change

The final means by which industrialized country abatement of greenhouse gases may affect other countries lies in a reduction in the rate of climatic change itself. The rate of climate change and the distribution and precise economic impacts of its effects are both subject to wide uncertainties. If abatement efforts are modest, so too will be the reduction in climate change. Nevertheless, some qualitative points about the effects can be made.

---

[2] (cont)
... *Positive Measures for Technology Transfer Under the Climate Change Convention* (London: RIIA, 1998).

Climate change is expected to affect most, perhaps all, developing countries adversely. They are likely to be more severely affected than most industrialized countries, both for physical reasons (they lie predominantly in regions that are already hotter and drier), and economic/institutional ones (poor countries more often have weak institutions and infrastructure, and generally low levels of technology, that make it more difficult to adapt to such changes). For most countries, the more rapid the rate of climate change, the more difficult and costly the adjustment process will be. Reducing the rate and degree of direct climate change impacts is the most obvious benefit to flow from industrialized country action to limit climate change.

As well as its direct domestic impacts, climate change will affect trade patterns. Like the impacts themselves, these are subject to wide uncertainties, but some qualitative aspects can be projected with reasonable confidence. Notably, one of the most consistent projections of climate models is that climate change will damage agricultural productivity in much of the developing world, so that many developing countries will become more dependent upon imports of agricultural products, particularly from northern countries, such as Canada and Russia, that may see improved agricultural output. The effect of industrialized country abatement in this respect is thus likely to be unambiguously beneficial to the great majority of developing countries.

2.5 Quantifying trade impacts

The complexities of international economic issues mean that they are generally studied using large-scale computer models, particularly general equilibrium (GE) models which seek to incorporate all three of the abatement issues discussed above (though they do not incorporate climatic impacts themselves).[3]

Most GE models suggest that constraints on CO_2 emissions in industrialized countries would impact negatively, in aggregate, upon the developing world. However, most such models model trade effects on

---

[3] See *The Use of Economic Models in Climate Policy Analysis* (EEP Climate Change Briefing No. 5, RIIA, 1997).

the basis of pre-Uruguay Round trade patterns and characteristics, which would tend to underestimate the responsiveness of trade to price differences, and many appear to overestimate the sensitivity of trade to income changes in the industrialized world.[4] Also, such models do not take account of the potential for 'no-regrets' measures that would reduce economic costs; and they do not model directly the impact of emission constraints on innovation. In these respects, they tend to exaggerate the negative economic impacts on developing countries. On the other hand, they assume that policies in industrialized countries are implemented simply as equivalent to a carbon tax, which probably exaggerates the benefits arising from industrial relocation to developing countries, as well as the disadvantages in terms of higher import prices.

Most of these studies do not present results in a way which enables the different components of impacts to be disentangled, or for specific national impacts to be evaluated. The Australian GETM model does present some specific national results, which tend to indicate significant losses for oil exporters (such as Indonesia and Mexico) and gains for several other developing countries (such as China, India and Korea; see Figure 2.3).[5] For the reasons given above, the non-energy trade impacts may well be exaggerated in such studies, so this highlights the extent to which the impacts on oil markets probably dominate the international economic repercussions of industrialized country action, at least for the level of commitments currently being considered. Countries that will be importing oil in 10 to 20 years – including the great majority of developing countries – are likely to gain marginal economic benefits, while oil exporters will tend to lose some revenue, as compared with base case growth. All these effects are small in comparison with the base case growth, but they help to explain the concerns of energy exporters, and the tensions within the developing world over the climate change issue.

---

[4] See chapter by N. Mabey, in Mabey et al., *Argument in the Greenhouse*.

[5] V. Tulpule, S. Brown, J. Lim, C. Polidano, H. Pam and B.S. Fisher, 'An Economic Assessment of the Kyoto Protocol Using the Global Trade and Environment Model', 27th Conference of Economists, Economics Society of Australia, University of Sydney, 28 September–1 October 1998.

Figure 2.3: Economic impact of uniform emission reductions on non-Annex I countries

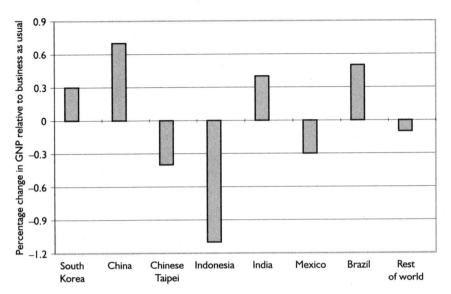

Source: Brown et al., *The Economic Impact of International Climate Change Policy*, ABARE, 1997.

Finally, modelling studies also highlight how the impacts depend upon how emissions reductions are implemented. Measures which reduce the costs to industrialized countries, such as emissions trading, will also reduce adverse impacts on developing countries. Furthermore, if emissions trading is extended to include developing countries, trade in emission quotas itself could become a source of revenue. Figure 2.4 shows the results of a study of the economic impacts of the proposal (for a 25 per cent reduction in emissions by 2005) made by the Alliance of Small Island States (AOSIS) in the run-up to the Kyoto conference of the parties, using MIT's EPPA model, in which developing countries are given quotas equal to their 'business-as-usual emissions.[6] In the first few decades, the ability to sell these quotas in return

---

[6] H.D. Jacobi, R.S. Eckhaus, A.D. Ellerman, R.G. Prinn, D.M. Reiner and Z. Yang, 'CO_2 emission limits: economic adjustments and the distribution of burdens', *The Energy Journal*, vol. 18, no. 3, 1997.

Figure 2.4: Discounted welfare loss to non-OECD regions over 2000–2050, with and without emissions trading

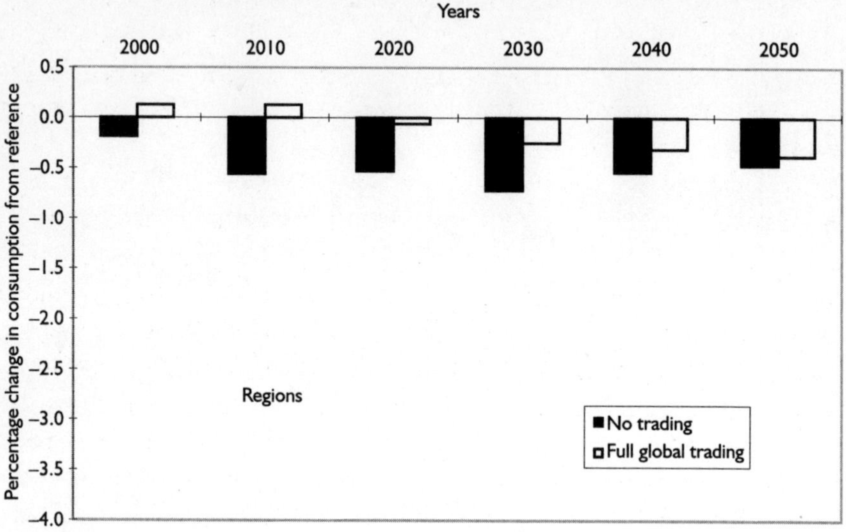

Source: Jacoby et al., 'CO$_2$ emission limits' (see footnote 6).

for low-cost domestic abatement produces net gains, and the overall greater efficiency of the system greatly reduces the adverse impacts to the middle of the century.

2.6 Emissions impact and 'leakage'

'Emissions leakage' refers to the possibility that action to limit emissions in industrialized countries will, as a consequence, lead to emission increases in countries not taking part in emission controls. This is potentially important because, to the extent that such leakage occurs, it clearly undermines the effectiveness of action taken by the industrialized countries. Estimates of leakage rates derived from modern general equilibrium models tend to suggest 'leakage' in the range 3–30 per cent – i.e. a 100 million tonne reduction of CO$_2$ in industrialized countries would increase emissions elsewhere by 3–30 million tonnes.[7]

---

[7] See IPCC, *Climate Change 1995: Economic and Social Dimensions of Climate Change*, p. 342 and pp. 424–5, and references therein. The IPCC also reports an 'outlier' result of

In most models, the biggest source of leakage arises from the impact on trade and the likely relocation of energy-intensive manufacturing. As noted, however, wherever abatement policies have been actively promoted, in practice governments have taken steps to exempt or rebate the impacts of their policies on internationally competitive energy-intensive industries. This negates a primary source of leakage in most modelling studies.

Furthermore – and especially in the longer term – technical change becomes as important a response to changes in domestic energy prices as does the possible relocation of investment and production. Emissions reduction measures in industrialized countries will tend to induce carbon-saving technical changes that will then diffuse internationally, leading to negative leakage – i.e. a reduction of emissions elsewhere because less carbon-intensive technologies will have become relatively more attractive globally. Although modellers have made their best efforts to mimic the effects of policies upon the rates of penetration of such new technologies, no economic models yet embody the effect of induced technical change on technology prices and global dissemination. Until models succeed in incorporating this, it is not really possible to guess even at the sign of the leakage, and it certainly cannot be assumed as a general principle that emission reductions in industrialized countries will lead to increased emissions elsewhere. Indeed, the opposite could occur, but as yet there is no way of quantifying this.

However, a recent study does illustrate that such effects could readily swamp the classical components of leakage.[8] The analysis considers the implications if international trade and economic integration lead ultimately to a convergence of emission intensities (ratio of emissions to GDP) between developed and developing countries. In this case, CO_2 abatement by the industrialized countries – which reduces their emis-

---

[7] (cont)
80% leakage that has subsequently been rescinded by the analyst involved (Pezzy, personal communication). Higher leakage rates still (exceeding 100%) have been postulated for some specific activities such as fertilizer production, but not overall.

[8] M. Grubb, 'Economic dimensions of technological and global responses to the Kyoto Protocol', *Journal of Economic Studies*, forthcoming winter 1999.

sions intensity – diffuses globally, implicitly (but not explicitly) reflecting the spread of more efficient technologies and practices. Table 2.1 shows resulting estimates of leakage, if the classical component of leakage is assumed to be 10 per cent, for varying degrees of such spillover, from none (0) to full convergence over the century (1). It is readily apparent such 'spillover' of low emission intensities can quickly swamp the classical component of leakage: by the end of the next century, indeed, emission reductions in the industralized countries are roughly matched by equivalent induced emission reductions in developing countries in the central (0.5) case, while in the case of full spillover/intensity convergence (1) they ultimately exert twice as much leverage.

Table 2.1: Summary of leakage results with convergence of emission intensities (%)

	2025	2050	2075	2100
No spillover ($\sigma=0$)	10	10	10	10
50% spillover ($\sigma=0.5$)	−25	−45	−76	−98
Complete spillover ($\sigma=1.0$)	−83	−125	−182	−206

Note: The table shows the negative of the ratio of changes of emissions in the developing countries to changes in industrialized country emissions (each relative to baseline), for different spillover assumptions given industrialized country emissions at Kyoto levels followed by a 1% annual reduction. Negative leakage indicates that the diffusion of lower emitting technologies and policies outweighs the classical component of leakage (e.g. from the migration of dirty industries), which is assumed to be 10%.

Source: Grubb, 'Economic dimensions of technological and global responses to the Kyoto Protocol'.

This is not so surprising. The international migration of heavy industry to escape emission controls is intrinsically limited. The international diffusion of induced technologies, practices and institutions can take purchase throughout a steadily expanding global market in which the developing economies are eventually larger than those of the industrialized world, giving a large multiplier effect. Such results are tentative and remain to be analysed further and more directly, but they do help to illustrate the central importance of understanding the international nature of the global economy, and the role of trade and investment in advanced and lower-emitting technologies within that. They also serve to highlight the potential importance of global trade-related aspects of the Protocol (for example, its provisions relating to technology transfer and the CDM).

2.7 Energy exporter impacts and 'compensation'[9]

Concerns about the potential impact of emission constraints upon energy trade led some energy exporting countries to oppose efforts to develop an agreement on emission constraints for a number of years. More recently, a number of oil exporters have proposed a 'compensation' mechanism for any lost revenues that might arise from emissions reduction measures.

Equivalent monetary compensation, however, would be hard to justify or even to define. The idea that commodity owners should be compensated for the loss of exports due to actions that reduce the demand by importers cannot be sustained as a general principle: resource owners do not automatically have a 'right' to exports of their commodity at any particular price or level. Should, for example, tobacco exporters be compensated for loss of sales if importers raise excise duties on tobacco, on health grounds, and thereby reduce demand?

However, as noted in Section 1.3, the Climate Convention does state that 'the Parties shall give full consideration to what actions are necessary under the Convention ... to meet the specific needs and concerns of the developing countries ... including ... (h) countries whose economies are highly dependent on income generated from ... fossil fuels.' This is part of a broader concern about the distributional impacts of climate change and of measures taken to limit it. While many oil exporters are relatively rich, as noted above, some are quite poor. Furthermore, it may simply be pragmatic politics to explore some ways to alleviate the concerns of energy exporters, much as domestic politics demands attention to the distributional impacts of policy changes.

---

[9] This section draws heavily upon results from Peter Kassler and Matthew Paterson, *Energy Exporters and Climate Change* (London: RIIA, 1997).

This need not, indeed cannot, take the form of direct monetary compensation for revenues lost by certain exporters due to emission constraints. To define the amount lost would require a knowledge of how international energy markets would have behaved in the absence of emission constraints: who would have exported how much at what price. This is clearly unknowable in detail.

Additional complications arise from recognizing the finite nature of energy reserves. Table 2.2 shows estimates of the reserves and estimated additional resources of gas, oil and coal. To reach an atmospheric concentration of 450ppm carbon dioxide – considered by many to be a relatively severe target – would, over the next century, require at least five times as much carbon to be emitted as exists in conventional proven oil reserves, or three times as much as in oil and gas reserves combined. Staying within the EU's proposed target of 550ppm would allow emissions of an amount of carbon 50 per cent higher again. Production from proven *conventional* oil reserves is expected to peak within about 20 years. Scenarios of long-term, large-scale atmospheric change derive their carbon from other sources: expansion of coal use, particularly for power generation (primarily domestic consumption in North America, China and India);[10] new discoveries of conventional oil and development of unconventional oil sources such as tar sands and oil shales; and new uses of coal, including synthetic fuels, to displace oil in premium markets as oil reserves deplete and costs rise.

This has important implications for climate change policy, beyond the scope of this book. It also has specific implications for the questions of economic impacts on exporters and 'compensation'. It highlights the fact that existing, proven reserves will be consumed almost regardless of climate change mitigation measures; they will affect the *rate* of consumption but not the total. Furthermore, in the longer term, actions to limit climate change may well inhibit other, new and more

---

[10] Total coal deposits are very large, but much of this is of poor quality and relatively difficult to access – such as most of the coal in Europe, that is now generally considered uneconomic. It is quite possible that the amount of carbon in low-cost coal deposits is as limited as in petroleum resources, but that is a very complex debate which is less relevant to the discussion here.

carbon-intensive developments (such as oil shales and synfuels from coal). In the longer term this may well make oil more valuable, not less. Long term modelling studies do suggest that oil producer prices would be higher in the long run with CO_2 constraints, and studies with the MIT's EPPA model predict that the cumulative net economic impact, discounted out to 2050, would be quite evenly spread between importers and exporters. The corollary of claims for near-term compensation for lost exports would thus be that exporters should pay back importers later on when prices rise owing to restraints on more carbon-intensive, competing sources – a proposition unlikely to be accepted by the proponents of compensation.

Table 2.2: Carbon contents for fossil fuels and atmospheric accumulation

Carbon in fossil fuel resources (Gtc)		
	Proven reserves	Additional resources
Conventional oil	120	36–110
Conventional gas	80	45–165
Coal	650	360–2300
Unconventional oil	142	180
Unconventional gas	105	35–270
Atmospheric accumulation		
Stabilization level		Allowable emissions 1990–2100 (Gtc)
450 ppm		630–650
550 ppm		870–990

Source: See Kassler and Paterson, Appendix 2.

Issues of climate change and energy resources are complex and intertwined, and both in part are matters of timing. Especially for countries with lower levels of oil resources, the issues are closely related to those of depletion policy, producer-consumer relations, and longer term diversification. Historically, oil markets have been subject to large and damaging swings and power shifts between producers and consumers. Long-run stability could benefit from cooperation, and assisting some oil exporters to address the implications of climate change as part of a political compromise in the negotiations could form part of that.

Kassler and Patterson[11] suggest that short-term options for political compromise could include: putting some fraction of carbon tax revenues towards economic adaptation in the more vulnerable countries; fiscal adjustments in consumer countries towards carbon-based taxes; discussion of offtake levels between major producers and consumers; enhanced investment in major producers by Annex I companies; explicit joint implementation/technology transfer projects; and joint R&D programmes. For the longer term, many oil exporters are rich in gas, depleted wells that could be used to dispose of separated CO_2, and/or renewable energy sources. Kassler and Patterson propose several options for assisting energy exporters to address the implications of climate change, including promotion of natural gas investment, joint development of CO_2 disposal techniques, cooperation towards techniques for low-emission hydrocarbon economies (such as hydrogen production, transport and use), and broader investment assistance for economic diversification.

2.8 Conclusions

Actions by industrialized countries to limit CO_2 emissions can affect other countries in several ways, including through impacts on international energy markets, trade in energy-intensive goods, overall trade structures and volumes, and reduced climatic impacts, particularly on agriculture. Economic modelling studies have sought to quantify the scale of the first three components, but at least for the level of commitments agreed at Kyoto probably exaggerate the scale of trade impacts. The most economically important internationally traded fuel is oil, but coal demand is likely to be far more affected than oil by the actions presently being contemplated.

Raising energy costs to energy-intensive manufacturing could result in these activities migrating to other countries, but precisely for that reason these sectors are likely to be shielded in one way or another. Reduced income in industrialized countries could reduce imports, but the models applied tend to neglect the scope for 'no-regret' measures

---

[11] Kassler and Paterson, *Energy Exporters and Climate Change*.

that reduce emissions without reducing aggregate income. Also, many such models appear to exaggerate income-related trade impacts and do not take adequate account of recent trade liberalization, thus potentially underestimating the extent to which price responses may offset income effects on international trade. Also, economic modelling studies neglect the offsetting benefits of climate change, which may be particularly important concerning agricultural impacts on developing countries. Overall impacts of international trade would include the international diffusion of the lower-carbon technologies that are likely to be developed in response to emission constraints in the industrialized world, and preliminary analysis suggests this could over time dominate the adverse components of 'leakage'.

On time scales of 10 to 20 years, the effects on oil markets, even if less than projected in the OPEC studies, appear likely to dominate other mechanisms. This implies a small net economic gain in terms of trade for the majority of developing countries, with losses concentrated upon the countries which depend primarily on oil or coal exports. Though direct financial compensation is neither technically nor politically feasible, various short-term and longer term measures could be explored, to minimize the impacts on exporters' revenue and to help these countries adjust. For the most part however, the effects of industrialized country action on other countries, both positive and negative, will be indistinguishable compared to the projected global growth in wealth and trade.

Chapter 3

Energy efficiency standards and trade

The application of minimum standards of energy efficiency, and of labels showing energy consumption, is becoming more widespread in countries aiming to reduce energy demand and emissions of carbon dioxide. This chapter explores the potential interaction between international trade and the application of such standards and labels at a national level.

3.1 Introduction: standards, labels and trade

Why energy efficiency standards?

There are two main grounds on which governments may wish to implement energy efficiency standards and/or energy labels: to reduce the external environmental impacts of energy consumption; and to correct failures in the way the market works.

In principle, a more cost-effective way of reducing environmental impacts would be to tax energy, raising its price to incorporate the costs of the environmental externalities associated with its use (including the impacts of climate change and of local and regional air pollution). In recent years a number of countries have indeed introduced energy or carbon taxes and/or have increased existing energy taxes (such as transport fuel excise duties) specifically for environmental reasons, and the topic has been much debated in several countries. There are, however, a number of problems with such environmental taxation, as the European and US experiences show (see further in Chapter 4). Any increase in taxation (particularly through a new tax) is almost invariably politically unpopular, both in the domestic sector, where low-income households may be particularly affected, and in the industrial sector, where international competitiveness effects are usually of perceived importance. Institutionally, environment ministries and agencies usually lack the clout within governments to persuade finance and industry ministries of the value of environmental taxes – and where energy taxes are introduced, it is usually for revenue purposes, not related to environmental objectives. Given these factors, energy labels and standards may often be seen as more attractive and feasible.[1]

In addition, there is widespread evidence that energy price signals do not result in the level of energy efficiency that might be expected if consumers were fully informed and acted to minimize costs. Information about, and awareness of, energy-saving opportunities and lifetime consumption costs are frequently lacking, especially in the domestic sector. Other preferences, such as performance or accessories for cars, for example, may be given a higher priority by consumers, manufacturers and retailers. The problem of lack of information can be countered by the application of *energy labelling*, showing the amount of energy a particular product consumes in use. Labels tend, however, to be of limited value. They usually indicate only energy consumption under defined testing conditions, rather than lifetime energy consumption, and consumers may still ignore or fail to interpret the information. Labelling may also be administratively costly and/or prone to abuse.

In these circumstances, the attraction of *minimum standards of energy efficiency* is obvious. In practice standards can be seen as correcting further for market failure, by lowering informational costs and removing the worst performing units from the market altogether. Although industry often dislikes the imposition of standards (along with government regulation in general), once applied they may be seen as helpful in maintaining a common floor for competition, ensuring that particular companies are not undercut by competitors, particularly those from overseas. The perceived political costs of introducing standards are much lower than the costs of the introduction or raising of energy taxation. Economic evaluation shows existing standards to be highly cost-

---

[1] The labels and standards in question relate to the energy consumed by the product *in use*. Labelling and standards programmes relating to the energy consumed in the *production process* of the products in question are also conceptually possible, and may become significant if concern over climate change grows – the ISO 14000 series (see below) provides a possible framework under which they could be developed. Since no such programmes exist as yet, however, the issues they might raise are not considered here.

effective, with the value of energy savings far exceeding the administrative and other identifiable costs.[2] For these reasons, and given the commitments to reduce greenhouse gas emissions embodied in the Kyoto Protocol, energy labels and standards seem likely to become more and more common, whether as voluntary initiatives or compulsory, government-mandated ones.

The interaction with trade

For traded products,[3] standards and labels can either be applied nationally or internationally. On the face of it, international harmonization would seem to make sense: common standards and labels should help to avoid trade barriers, mitigate competitiveness problems (from any costs of higher standards) and contribute to greater consumer awareness and understanding. Mainly for this reason, many of the policies and measures proposed for consideration in the negotiations on the Kyoto Protocol (and ended up as Article 2 of the agreement) envisaged the international harmonization of standards. This causes, however, potential problems:

- The negotiation of international standards is usually a long process requiring considerable effort, and it may be difficult to reach agreement on anything other than very low standards.
- Common standards may not always be appropriate to different countries. The present climate change abatement commitments apply only to industrialized countries, but are likely eventually to be extended to developing countries, whose industries may face greater costs in adapting to higher standards.

---

[2] See, for example, Fiona Mullins, *Demand Side Efficiency: Energy Efficiency Standards for Traded Products* (Paris: IEA/OECD, 1996; Annex I Expert Group on the UN FCCC, 'Policies and Measures for Common Action', Working Paper 5), pp. 55–8. Cost savings may not always be apparent to the consumer where energy production is subsidized, since they face artificially low prices.

[3] Buildings are one of the main areas for the application of energy efficiency standards – but since they are not traded, there is little case for harmonization and no impact on trade. Some building materials that affect efficiency might, however, be traded.

- Even among industrialized countries, circumstances differ; an appliance running on electricity generated mainly from renewable or nuclear sources, for example, will have a very different impact on climate change than one running on coal-generated electricity.

Setting standards and labels only at a national level may also, however, cause potential problems:

- Market access barriers may arise from different standards and labelling requirements in different countries.
- Similar trade barriers may arise from difficulties in accessing the testing and certification systems required by the importing country, and the costs of multiple test protocols.
- There may be constraints imposed by the multilateral trading system (the GATT, and its associated agreements, administered by the WTO).
- There may be a loss of international competitiveness in the country enforcing higher standards, if costs to its exporters are raised as a result.

The first two of these points were in fact cited as causing potential trade barriers to goods produced in developing countries by a number of parties (including India, Korea, Morocco and Egypt) in the negotiations on the Kyoto Protocol.[4]

Labels and standards in practice

The debate around energy efficiency and trade revolves around the following instruments: [5]

---

[4] James Cameron et al., 'Implementing the Climate Change Convention: Trade Law Implications on the Road to Kyoto and Beyond' (Foundation for International Environmental Law and Development (FIELD) for Global Environment and Trade Study (GETS), 1998).

[5] Definitions taken from OECD/IEA, 'Improving product efficiency through ratings, labels, targets and regulatory standards' (Paris: OECD/IEA, 1996), and John Duffy, *Energy Labeling, Standards and Building Codes: a Global Survey and Assessment for Selected Developing Countries* (Washington DC: International Institute for Energy Conservation, 1996).

- *Labels* refer to product listings and markings showing models' energy use or efficiency. *Comparison* labelling programmes provide consumers with information to compare all products within a given category. *Endorsement* labelling programmes identify and endorse a limited number of products that meet a specified high efficiency standard.
- *Standards* refer to regulations stipulating the minimum energy performance standards for products sold in a particular country or region. *Minimum performance standards* are set by governments and are mandatory; they are typically set at levels that lower product life cycle costs without compromising product performance and features. *Voluntary high performance standards* define a high efficiency threshold and are used to determine eligibility for endorsement labelling programmes or other energy conservation initiatives. Standards normally apply to every product in a particular category on the market, but coverage can occasionally apply to a given percentage of products or a market-wide or manufacturer-based average.
- *Test protocols* provide the necessary base for developing labels and standards. In general, they are designed to be relatively simple, reproducible, and representative of actual operating conditions – though the last factor embodies a great deal of uncertainty about user behaviour, equipment options, external climate, and so on. The responsibility for developing and maintaining test protocols normally resides with trade associations or national and regional standards organizations, rather than governments. ISO (the International Organization for Standardization), a federation of national standards bodies, and its sister organization the International Electrotechnical Commission, have developed a number of test protocols, but, at least in the area of energy efficiency, no labels or standards. The ISO 14000 series of environmental management standards, however, has the potential to develop relevant standards, possibly including energy use during production.

Energy efficiency labels and standards are gradually becoming more widespread. This is the case particularly in the US, where they cover 13 categories of major domestic appliances. The (voluntary) Energy Star labelling scheme for computers and other office equipment has

---

Box 3.1: Greenhouse gas emissions reductions potential: refrigerators/freezers

Region	Carbon savings			
	'Introductory' scenario		'More rigorous' scenario	
	Mt-CO_2	%	Mt-CO_2	%
Western Europe	3	6	12	24
North America	–	–	10	13
Japan	0.5	7	3	37
Central & eastern Europe	2	14	2.5	18
CIS	2	23	3	45
All regions	7	5	30	18

The table illustrates the potential reduction in carbon dioxide emissions from base (which itself assumes some improvements, mainly through new stock replacing old) by 2010, for two scenarios for the introduction of stricter energy efficiency standards for refrigerators/freezers.

- An 'introductory' level equivalent to the proposed EU standards (note that this has no effect in North America as standards are already higher there).
- A 'more rigorous' level equivalent to the highest level adopted in any country in the near future (the proposed US NAECA (Natural Appliance Energy Conservation Act) standards, originally expected to take effect in 1998 but delayed).

For comparison, emissions from refrigerators/freezers in 1995 were 188 Mt-CO_2 for all regions; this is expected to fall to 160 Mt-CO_2 in 2010 (base case). Refrigeration represents the largest electricity end-use in the domestic sector; typically about 20% of domestic consumption.

Source: Fiona Mullins, *Demand Side Efficiency* (see footnote 2), pp. 32–41

---

become so widely adopted (internationally as well as domestically) as to become virtually a *de facto* standard. Automobile fuel economy is regulated through fiscal instruments, including the 'gas guzzler' tax and the Corporate Average Fuel Economy (CAFE) regulations. The EU started to introduce energy labelling requirements for domestic appliances from 1995 (initially for refrigerators). A minimum standard for refrigerators related to the labelling code (level C in the current scale) will be introduced in September 1999. Discussions with vehicle manufacturers resulted in a voluntary agreement on car fuel economy standards in October 1998 (see below, section 3.3).

Elsewhere, standards and labels for domestic appliances are fairly common in the industrialized world, and a number of developing countries, including Korea, Thailand, Brazil and Mexico, also possess such programmes. Box 3.1 indicates the potential for carbon savings deriving from the application of standards in one sector.

3.2 Trade barriers

Trade barriers: standards and labels

The potential for trade barriers arising from different national standards is obvious; exporters, particularly those from developing countries or transition economies, may find it difficult to meet the standards applied by industrialized countries with more advanced industries and more developed legislation. While this may be true in theory, neither a literature search nor a wide range for interviews carried out for this project have been able to discover any evidence for it in practice.

This finding is supported by other instances of environmental regulation affecting trade. The Montreal Protocol on Substances that Deplete the Ozone Layer, for example, applies different phase-out schedules for controlled substances such as chlorofluorocarbons (CFCs) as between developed and developing countries. While the main categories of CFCs were phased out completely in the developed world by the beginning of 1996 (apart from a few approved exemptions), developing countries can continue to produce and consume them until 2010. Yet exports of affected products from developing to developed countries appear not to have been particularly adversely affected. While the Chinese export trade in refrigerators containing CFCs fell between 1988 and 1991, for example, Chinese manufacturers who had switched to CFC-free technologies saw their exports increase.[6] Studies in Malaysia revealed little or no effect on the refrigeration and air-conditioning industry, with unit prices rising only in line with raw material costs. In general, developing country exports to OECD countries of refrigerators have grown much more rapidly than intra-OECD trade in

---

[6] United Nations Environment Programme (UNEP), *1994 Report of the Economic Options Committee* (Nairobi: UNEP, 1994), pp. 6–10.

such products.[7] A study in Thailand showed that exports of electronics items continued to grow at about 30 per cent per year before and after phase-out of CFC solvents.[8]

The conclusion that energy efficiency standards and labels do not present serious barriers to trade is not, perhaps, too surprising, when the levels of the standards and labels themselves are considered. Existing energy efficiency standards, and those currently under consideration in various quarters, do not in general even closely approach the best available technology; they tend to underpin, rather than stretch, efficiency levels.

Indeed, there appears to be no consistent relationship between cost and efficiency levels for many products: more efficient goods are not necessarily more costly to buy.[9] Manufacturers are constantly changing and modifying their product lines in response to actual or perceived consumer tastes, technological developments and supplies and costs of raw materials as well as government regulations. Incorporating energy efficiency standards, which tend to be raised only gradually over time, has caused no real problems, particularly for dynamic industries used to rapid innovation, such as PCs. Even in developing countries and transition economies, it can be concluded that manufacturers who are capable of producing goods of a high enough quality for export are in general capable of conforming to what are in reality relatively low standards of energy efficiency.

When, or if, standards ever do begin to approach levels that involve serious trade-offs between energy efficiency and capital costs, and if

---

[7] United Nations Conference on Trade and Development (UNCTAD), *Effects of Environmental Policies, Standards and Regulations on Market Access and Competitiveness,* 28 March 1995 (TD/B/WG.6/6); UNCTAD, *Environment, International Competitiveness and Development: Lessons from Empirical Studies: The Policy Debate on Trade, Environment and Development,* 12 September 1995.

[8] *Thailand and the Montreal Protocol: Assessing Progress and Impacts* (draft report submitted to UNCTAD by the Thailand Environment Institute, 1997).

[9] See, for example, Brenda Boardman et al., *Transforming the UK Cold Market* (Oxford: Environmental Change Unit, Oxford University, 1997), which found 'no relationship between efficiency and price' for fridge-freezers (p. 24), a finding confirming those of many other studies in Europe and North America. Mullins, *Demand Side Efficiency,* found the costs of adding Energy Star features to PCs to be 'negligible' (p. 56).

they are raised more frequently, it is conceivable that greater market access barriers may be created – but at least until that happens, the relationship between standards and trade may in reality prove beneficial to the environment. Companies exporting to regions with energy efficiency standards may in practice raise standards in their domestic markets as well, as economies of scale in general encourage them to maintain single product lines. There is some evidence that that has already happened in the case of refrigerator manufacture in central and eastern European countries which are aspiring EU entrants. Thus trade can help higher standards to spread. Once again, this is a conclusion supported by other examples of environmental regulation. The US introduction of gradually lower vehicle emission limits for nitrogen oxides in the 1970s and 1980s, for example, helped to persuade German car manufacturers (with relatively large volumes of exports) to lobby for similar regulations within the EU.[10]

Where *ranges* of products are manufactured, however, as is often the case, the lower efficiency end of the range may be maintained for the domestic market. There is evidence of this happening in Hungary and Slovenia, and also in South America, where US-owned plants export higher efficiency products to North America, but sell lower quality goods in their host countries.[11] Thus the impact of efficiency standards outside the importing market may be limited.

Trade barriers: testing and certification systems

Access to testing and certification systems pose, again, obvious potential problems, and may impose additional administrative costs where such systems differ between markets. The three big regional refrigerator markets, for example (western Europe, North America and Japan) employ different testing protocols to arrive at energy consumption figures. The case for harmonization of testing protocols is clearly the stronger the more global the market.

---

[10] See David Wallace, *Environmental Policy and Industrial Innovation: Strategies in Europe, the US and Japan* (London: RIIA/Earthscan, 1995), p. 151.
[11] Andrew Gilchrist and Melanie Slade (Energy Technology Support Unit), personal communication.

In practice, however, exporters do not appear to experience serious trade barriers as a result. Many labelling systems, such as the EU energy label, only require self-certification by the manufacturer, so the exporter only needs to obtain the relevant information from the EU authorities – there is no requirement for the product to be tested externally before it may be placed on the market.[12] Similarly, the US Environmental Protection Agency has proved cooperative in providing the necessary information to foreign manufacturers to comply with the Energy Star label.

Trade barriers: the multilateral trading system

As described in Chapter 1, the central aims of the multilateral trading system are to liberalize trade and to prevent discrimination between members of the WTO. The Technical Barriers to Trade (TBT) Agreement, negotiated in 1979 and extended in the 1994 Uruguay Round, regulates the use of national technical regulations and standards which could influence international trade, including characteristics relating to production methods, and issues such as packaging and labelling requirements. The main purpose of the TBT Agreement is to ensure that the use of technical regulations (mandatory), product standards (voluntary) and conformity assessment procedures do not create unnecessary barriers to trade. Such standards are to be transparent, non-discriminatory, and no more trade-restrictive than necessary to fulfil a legitimate objective, which is defined as including, *inter alia,* 'protection of human health or safety, animal or plant life or health, or the environment'.[13] The Agreement encourages countries to use international standards where possible (for example, ISO standards), but creates no requirement to harmonize domestic regulations and standards. Of the 400–500 technical barriers notified to the WTO Secretariat every year because they might cause significant trade effects – of which

---

[12] This may of course compromise the effectiveness of the label. Competing manufacturers can probably be relied upon to verify their competitors' claims, and in fact some EU national authorities (though by no means all) do test the products.

[13] Agreement on Technical Barriers to Trade, Article 2.2.

energy efficiency standards are an important category – none has ever been challenged as being unnecessarily trade-restrictive.

There has, however, been one case of a serious trade conflict involving energy efficiency standards: the 1993–4 US–EC dispute over taxes on automobiles, usually known as the 'CAFE case'. In March 1993, the European Community filed a case against the United States, claiming that three car taxes applied by the US violated international trade rules in that they discriminated against US imports of European cars. The GATT disputes panel established to investigate the case ruled that two of the taxes – the luxury tax, and the 'gas guzzler' tax aimed at cars with a fuel consumption less than 22.5mpg – were GATT-consistent since they were not applied in a discriminatory way; they applied equally to all cars, wherever they were manufactured.

The other part of the dispute dealt with the CAFE standards, which require car manufacturers to achieve an average fuel efficiency of at least 27.5 mpg across their entire fleet. The panel ruled that the application of the regulations only to that portion of the European manufacturers' fleets that were imported into the US (which tended to be high-value, low-efficiency products) was GATT-inconsistent. Higher-efficiency cars produced in the EU but not exported to the US were not allowed to be offset against the lower-efficiency models that were exported. European manufacturers were therefore treated less favourably than US ones; this was discriminatory, and therefore GATT-illegal.

The multilateral trading system should therefore pose no objections to the pursuit of energy efficiency objectives, provided that these are not implemented in a discriminatory manner – and it is difficult to think of any *environmental* reason why they should be. It should be noted, however, that as the GATT is essentially a proscriptive agreement, defining what contracting parties may not do (or may do under certain circumstances), interpretation proceeds through a case law-type approach, following rulings by dispute panels in particular cases. Since there has not yet been a dispute case involving the TBT Agreement, it is impossible to predict precisely how a dispute panel might interpret the phrase 'unnecessary obstacle to international trade' in Article 2.5. Whereas complainants in a number of cases have cited breach of the TBT Agreement as one of their justifications, the panels have in practice decided the case on breaches of other agreements, usually the GATT itself. One dispute involving the TBT Agreement is, at the time of writing, under way – the Canada–EC dispute on asbestos and asbestos products – and a number of other cases still in the consultation stage may involve the Agreement. However, various disputes panels – such as that dealing with the first tuna-dolphin case in 1991 – have commented approvingly on the use of labels, as non-discriminatory consumer-based alternatives to trade barriers.[14]

Another WTO dispute over vehicle fuel efficiency standards threatened to erupt during 1999, as European car manufacturers responded to Japanese proposals to modify domestic taxes on the basis of fuel efficiency. The Council for Transport Policy (a government advisory body) suggested that lowering the rates of two of the eight taxes currently applied to vehicles in Japan – on possession and on weight – for vehicles of small engine size and high fuel efficiency would be helpful in meeting Japan's commitments under the Kyoto Protocol; it called for tax changes in 2000. In a repeat of the CAFE case, European manufacturers noted that almost 90 per cent of European car sales in Japan fell into the three medium- to heavyweight categories which would be most severely affected.

The story was complicated, however, by the simultaneous talks between the European Car Manufacturers' Association (ACEA) and the Japan Automobile Manufacturers' Association (JAMA) (and the Korean Automobile Manufacturers' Association, KAMA) over the introduction of similar voluntary standards for CO_2 emissions from passenger vehicles as ACEA had agreed with the European Commission in late 1998 (see below, section 3.3). Facing slow progress in the talks, in June EU environment ministers threatened restrictions on Japanese car imports if agreement was not reached by September. In turn, JAMA pointed out that a relatively high proportion of Japanese car exports to Europe fell into the large-size, low-efficiency categories, partly because the EU levy on car imports made it uneconomic to export smaller, cheaper ones.

---

[14] In the tuna-dolphin case, the panel found that the US 'dolphin-safe' labelling scheme was compatible with GATT requirements – and it proved to be highly effective, removing much unlabelled product from the marketplace.

Although ACEA spokesmen were quick to suggest the threat of a WTO challenge against Japan, given the tangled, but almost mirror-image situation in which both trading blocs disproportionately export low-efficiency vehicles to each other, it seems unlikely that the EU would in reality pursue this course of action. And, as in the CAFE case, as long as the various standards and taxes were applied in a non-discriminatory manner to domestic and foreign products alike, there seems no reason to believe that such a challenge would succeed.

Competitiveness concerns

The remaining issue covers the area of international competitiveness. If countries impose energy efficiency standards unilaterally, does this impose costs on its manufacturers, such that exports become less competitive in international markets? As in the case of trade barriers against imports, literature surveys and interviews reveal no evidence that this has been the case or is likely to be. At the levels at which standards are applied at present, producers do not incur significant additional costs; indeed as noted, there is in general no clear relationship between manufacturing cost and product energy efficiency in any case. The imposition of mandatory standards may only become a matter of concern if they are applied in an unpredictable and arbitrary way, with little time to adjust existing product lines.

Furthermore, as noted above, most products are produced in a range of models, and manufacturers may continue to export the lower-efficiency versions to markets with less strict standards. Within the EU refrigerator industry, for example, UK consumers tend to buy lower-efficiency models and German consumers higher ones, irrespective of standards and labels. The issue is complicated further by the changing nature of international trade. Increasingly, and particularly for larger products such as cars, it is investment rather than trade which shifts in response to new markets. A US, European or Japanese car manufacturer may now be more likely to open a new plant, or joint venture, in a country with a growing market than export more finished units to it; hence the presence of efficiency standards in its 'home' market is less relevant.

3.3 The politics of setting standards

It appears to be the case, then, that the imposition of energy efficiency standards and labels does not in practice create trade barriers or adverse competitiveness effects, at least at the relatively low levels at which they are currently applied. The best available technology for domestic appliances in the EU, for example, shows a reduction in electricity consumption of about 40–50 per cent compared to the existing average,[15] and for cars about 30–40 per cent (or much higher with radical redesigns).[16] This in turn raises the question of *why* standards should be so low. Possible answers include:

- Manufacturer resistance to government regulation – true more of standards than of labels, which may sometimes be welcomed as encouraging recognition for exports (particularly true for Energy Star) – though energy labelling regulation in the EU was opposed for many years.
- Lack of consumer and retailer interest, reinforced by low world energy prices and inadequate public promotion campaigns.

Manufacturers tend to resist the setting of mandatory efficiency standards partly because of the potential administrative costs of compliance, but the strongest opposition generally comes from manufacturers who would have to change their current practice and product lines to comply. Even if meeting the standards would not make goods less competitive, they would still face retooling costs. And even if the retooling costs are in reality minimal, manufacturers often seem to fear the start of a process which may mean increased costs in the future, as governments progressively raise the standards.

A good example of industry's aversion to government-mandated standards is provided by recent developments in car fuel efficiency

---

[15] Department of Science, Technology and Society, Utrecht University, *Policies and Measures to Reduce CO_2 Emissions by Efficiency and Renewables* (Utrecht: World Wide Fund for Nature, 1996), p. 73.

[16] Claire Holman, 'Clean and Efficient Cars', in Michael Grubb et al, *Emerging Energy Technologies* (London: Royal Institute of International Affairs/Dartmouth Publishing, 1992).

standards in Europe. In October 1998, ACEA announced an agreement with the European Commission for a significant reduction of CO_2 emissions from new passenger cars sold in the EU – an average target of 140 gCO2/km (about 6l fuel/100km) for new passenger cars by the year 2008, representing a reduction of 25 per cent compared to 1995. While welcoming the agreement, the Commission announced that it would consider introducing binding legislation if the target was not met.

This manufacturer resistance is important in the political process of setting standards, which generally involves negotiating with manufacturers and their trade associations. It tends to drive their level down towards the lowest common denominator amongst the main manufacturers involved, and to make the process of ratcheting up standards very slow. Industry resistance may decline as climate change becomes more widely accepted as a major issue and if other measures – such as energy taxation – are seen as less palatable alternatives, but it will still be an important influence, and one that varies greatly across countries.

This also has important implications for the question of whether standards should be harmonized from the outset. In the US, the development of energy efficiency standards has been led by individual states (particularly California). Manufacturers of inefficient products based in other states could not block such standards. After a number of states had introduced them, the manufacturers tended to accept the need to retool to produce more efficient products, and indeed in some cases started to support the development of harmonized federal standards so as to avoid the administrative costs and complexity of meeting different requirements in different states.

In the EU, by contrast, the emphasis has been upon trying to harmonize efficiency standards from the outset. As a result, progress has been painfully slow. The country with the least efficient manufacturing industry has tended to exert undue influence and frequently has sought to stop the process moving forward significantly. Measures to promote energy efficiency have been under serious discussion since the mid 1970s, but only in the early 1990s did the EU succeed in introducing energy labelling, and the first energy efficiency standards are only now beginning to enter force. Such experience should raise extreme caution about proposals to try and harmonize global standards under the Kyoto Protocol.

3.4 Conclusions

As a general conclusion, it would appear to be the case that at least current energy efficiency standards and labels, and their associated testing and certification systems, pose few if any barriers to trade; that there is little likelihood of future conflict with the multilateral trading system; and that competitiveness concerns have no real foundation.

What does this imply for future negotiations on the climate change regime? The lists of policies and measures proposed by various parties during the negotiations leading up to Kyoto all included the development of energy efficiency standards and labelling, including various proposals for harmonization, coordination, and so on. Article 2 of the Protocol includes 'enhancement of energy efficiency in relevant sectors of the national economy'[17] as one of the areas in which parties should implement policies and measures to reduce greenhouse gas emissions.

Clearly trade barriers would be minimized, if not eliminated, by harmonized standards, labels and test protocols. There are, however, serious objections to the *harmonization* of *standards*. These include:

- Product standards are static instruments that can act to frustrate dynamic and innovative developments (well-designed programmes incorporate regular reviews and revisions, but this may be very difficult to achieve in a multilateral context).
- Standards will often need to vary with factors such as consumer preferences (for example, refrigerator size), climate (for example, lighting) or other national regulations (for example, vehicle fuel taxes, speed limits).
- Monitoring and enforcement costs could be significant given the large number of products regulated, the rate of technological innovation and the complex technical nature of the standards. Many

---

[17] Kyoto Protocol, Article 2 (1) (a) (i)

countries may simply lack the institutional capacity to enforce standards.
- The time and effort needed to negotiate standards on the part of policy-makers can be substantial. One study suggests that the time needed for researching, planning and negotiating common standards at Annex I level could be about five years,[18] a conclusion which appears optimistic given the length of time needed within the EU to agree even the energy label regulations (though the US experience suggests that if there is the political will, and flexibility for individual states to set higher standards, programmes can proceed more smoothly).

Given the potential for trade to spread higher standards, it seems logical to conclude that the costs of trying to agree common energy efficiency standards across any more than a small group of countries outweigh the benefits, though clearly the development and evolution of stronger *national* standards should be encouraged. This conclusion is stronger the larger the market and the greater the extent of trade in the product in question.

There is a much stronger case for attempting to harmonize *labelling requirements* and *testing procedures*, in order to reduce the bureaucracy and costs involved in exporting to different destinations. Even here, however, regional and national differences such as climate, product service characteristics and behavioural and product usage patterns need to be taken into account. Within the climate change regime, this could in theory be a role for the Subsidiary Body on Scientific and Technical Advice, or any technology assessment panels that may be set up under it, working together with existing international bodies such as the International Standards Organization.

Finally, energy efficiency regulations should not be applied in a discriminatory way to avoid clashes with the multilateral trading system – but, as noted above, there is no environmental case for doing so anyway.

---

[18] Mullins, *Demand Side Efficiency*, p. 65.

Chapter 4

Energy pricing and trade

The price of energy to its final user is a key determinant of the demand for its use. The price of carbon-based fuels – coal, oil and gas – is therefore an important influence on emissions of carbon dioxide. Governments can exert influence on the prices produced by the market in a number of ways: through increasing competition by market liberalization, by providing or removing subsidies for energy production or consumption, and by applying taxation (based on energy, carbon content or a mixture of both). All these actions can also have impacts (real or perceived) on the international competitiveness of business in the country in question (see Chapter 2) and specific policy instruments may be applied to mitigate any such negative impacts. This chapter examines these issues and their interaction with the multilateral trading system.

4.1 Energy and carbon taxes

The taxation of energy use or of carbon emissions as a policy option to mitigate climate change is increasingly being considered by industrialized countries. Indeed, Article 2 of the Kyoto Protocol (see Chapter 1) commits parties to implement 'progressive reduction or phasing out of market imperfections, fiscal incentives, tax and duty exemptions and subsidies in all greenhouse gas emitting sectors that run counter to the objective of the Convention and application of market instruments'.[1] A number of countries, mainly in northern Europe, have already introduced energy or carbon taxes for explicitly environmental reasons (often as part of a wider scheme of environmental tax reform), and almost every country, of course, taxes some categories of fossil fuels (usually oil and its derivatives) for revenue

---

[1] Kyoto Protocol, Article 2.1(a)(v).

purposes. The sums involved may be quite significant; in 1993 for example, Denmark derived approximately 7 per cent and Norway more than 10 per cent of total tax revenues from environment-related taxes.[2]

Table 4.1: Energy taxes in selected European countries

Country	Tax	Heavy fuel oil (£/1000 kg)	Natural gas (pence/m³)	Coal (£/1,000 kg)	Electricity (pence/kWh)
Austria	Energy	26.2	3.5	0	0.6
Denmark	Carbon	30.1	2.1	22.8	10
Finland	Carbon	37.6	1.2	28.9	4.1
Netherlands	Carbon/energy	0	21.3*	0	3
	Energy	10.3	10.5*	7.4	0
Norway	Carbon	34.9	n/a	34.2	0
Sweden	Carbon	44	3.1	34.6	0
	Energy	57.2	1.8	23.5	11.5

Source: Economic Instruments and the Business Use of Energy (report by Lord Marshall to the UK Treasury, November 1998), p. 41.

Tax rates are from 1997 except Finland and Denmark (1998) and are highest applicable (reduced rates are levied in certain conditions).

* £/tonne liquefied petroleum gas (LPG).

This section summarizes recent experience with energy and/or carbon taxation in various economies, particularly in Europe. All EU countries tax the use of mineral oil in the economy, with the exceptions of marine and aviation bunker fuels (see Chapter 5). There are, however, a number of specific exemptions for particular industries or sectors, including in the production of aluminium in Ireland and Italy; and Denmark and Sweden have a derogation from the Commission to apply lower taxation on fuels used in the industrial sector. Germany and Italy tax the use of natural gas, Austria and France tax gas and electricity, Denmark, Finland, The Netherlands and Sweden impose taxes on natural gas, coal and electricity use, and the UK is set to introduce an en-

---

[2] Organization for Economic Cooperation and Development, *Environmental Taxes in OECD Countries* (Paris: OECD, 1995).

ergy tax on business from 2001. Norway, a non-EU country, has imposed a carbon tax on business. Such evidence as is available suggests that such taxes can contribute to the reduction of carbon dioxide emissions.

The most far-reaching energy/carbon taxes have been introduced in Austria, Denmark, Finland, The Netherlands, Norway and Sweden (see Table 4.1 for a summary of tax rates), and are proposed in Germany and the UK. There have also been attempts to introduce such taxes at an EU level.[3]

European Community

The 1992 the European Commission proposed an EC-wide carbon/energy tax, applied to all energy sources, excluding renewables, with the intention of internalizing the costs of all environmental externalities, not just those associated with greenhouse gas emissions. The tax was to be applied on a 50:50 basis by energy and carbon content. It was to be introduced at a level of $3 per barrel of oil equivalent and increased in one-dollar steps over seven years, to reach a final level of $10/boe. The revenue raised by the tax was to be recycled into the economy; member states were to choose the precise routes. Although the initial tax level was quite low, the final addition to costs would be significant: coal prices were projected to increase (on average across all member states) by 63 per cent, gas by 31 per cent for industry and 13 per cent for households, electricity by 15 per cent and 13 per cent and transport fuel by 6–9 per cent.

Steps were taken in the design of the tax to protect industry from negative competitiveness impacts. The tax was to be applied 'downstream', to consumption rather than production. This is a sensible

---

[3] Information in this section is largely drawn from Richard Baron, *Annex I Expert Group on the UNFCCC: Policies and Measures for Common Action, Working Paper 4 – Economic/Fiscal Instruments: Taxation (i.e. Carbon/Energy)* (Bonn: UNFCCC, 1996), Mikael Skou Andersen and Duncan Liefferink, *The New Member States and the Impact on Environmental Policy* (Aarhus University, 1996) and Kai Schlegelmilch, *Energy Taxation in the EU and some Member States: Looking for Opportunities Ahead* (Wuppertal Institute, 1998).

measure to avoid raising domestic energy prices (for example, for electricity) while seeing imports unaffected, but it weakened the environmental impact, which would have been greater if electricity inputs had been taxed. In addition, energy-intensive firms were to be protected against competition from outside the EC: member states were to be permitted to refund part of the tax in proportion to a firm's energy costs when they exceeded 10 per cent of total costs, and the whole of the tax in the case of firms whose energy costs made up more than 20 per cent of production costs.

Finally, the adoption of the tax was to be conditional on other major OECD economies – which in practice meant the US and Japan – adopting similar measures. In the light of their failure to do so, and also after fierce opposition from some member states (alarmed either by the principle of raising energy prices or by the loss of sovereignty implicit in EC-level taxation) the proposal was effectively abandoned.

The Commission developed various further proposals, of which the latest is the draft Energy Products Directive, a plan to extend, throughout the EU, existing minimum excise rates and legislation on mineral oils to all energy products (apart from renewables) and to increase these minimum excise rates in three steps in 1998, 2000 and 2002. Once again, energy-intensive firms (defined here as companies spending more than 10 per cent of production costs on fuel) were to be granted partial or total exemptions. The impact on individual member states varied depending on their existing tax structures: Denmark, Finland, Sweden and Italy would be least affected, and Ireland, Spain, Belgium and Luxembourg most. Even this far weaker proposal proved controversial and has not yet been adopted. In February 1999 the European Parliament sent the proposal back to committee for further debate, their opposition springing from a coalition of groups feeling that the proposals were not radical enough with others who felt they were too extreme.

Austria

Austria introduced an energy tax on natural gas and electricity in 1996. The total tax burden for energy-intensive firms was capped at 0.35 per cent of the net value of production for manufacturing industry, and the tax was not applied to gas used in generation or to small autogenerators. The revenue (Sch3 billion in 1996, projected Sch7 billion in 1997) was directed towards general government expenditure, but partly earmarked for energy-saving measures (Sch690 million in 1997) and public transport (Sch730 million in 1997).

Further environmental tax proposals are under development for implementation possibly in 2000 or 2001. These include possible taxes on flights, water extraction, waste, and further taxes on energy and on the use of revenue for the reduction of labour costs and for energy-efficiency investments.

Denmark

In Denmark a tax on household energy use – which was broadly based upon the energy content of the fuel – has been in place since 1977. The concept was extended in 1993, in light of slow progress with the EU tax, through the introduction of a CO_2 tax on energy consumption as part of a package including subsidies for less carbon-intensive fuels and energy efficiency. The CO_2 tax was imposed upon all types of carbon dioxide emission sources, with the exception of petroleum, natural gas and biofuels, and was differentiated in proportion to the carbon dioxide content of each fuel. The overall rate was DKr100 ($14.9)/$tCO_2$, with a 50 per cent reimbursement for business generally available (with further reimbursements for those firms that paid a disproportionate tax relative to total taxable income).

In 1996 a more comprehensive tax scheme was introduced which imposed three different tax rates:

- On 'heavy industry' (a negotiated list of energy-intensive firms and firms operating in internationally competitive markets) – DKr5/tCO_2 growing to DKr25 ($3.7)/$tCO_2$ between 1996 and 2000; if the firm

implements a voluntary agreement to improve energy efficiency, the rate is reduced to $DKr3/tCO_2$.
- On all other industry – $DKr50/tCO_2$ growing to DKr90 ($13.4)/$tCO_2$ between 1996 and 2000; a voluntary agreement to improve energy efficiency reduces the rate to $DKr68/tCO_2$.
- On energy use for space heating – $DKr200/tCO_2$ growing to DKr600 ($89)/$tCO_2$ between 1996 and 2000; this is equivalent to the sum of the carbon and energy taxes applied in the household sector in 1996.

For trade reasons, electricity is exempt from the carbon tax; a subsidy for the use of gas in electricity generation is available to encourage fuel switching from coal.

In 1993 the total net revenue of the tax amounted to more than DKr3 million (about $0.5m). Carbon tax revenue from industry is entirely recycled to that sector, though lower employers' social contributions, investment grants for energy efficiency improvements (up to 30 per cent of the initial outlay) and special treatment for small businesses. The net impact of the tax plus revenue recycling in various ways is estimated to reduce carbon dioxide emissions by 4.7 per cent from 1988 to 2000, and a net positive impact on employment is expected from the tax recycling.

Finland

In 1990 Finland introduced Europe's first explicit carbon tax, imposed on all fossil fuels in proportion to their carbon content. The tax was initially set at the relatively low level of Mk24.5 ($1.2)/$tCO_2$ and was incorporated as a surtax on the pre-existing excise duty on fossil fuels. In 1993 the tax rate was doubled to $Mk50/tCO_2$, with a tax differentiation for diesel and petrol. The tax had only a modest impact on fuel prices: the price of electricity and natural gas increased by 1–2 per cent, coal, petroleum and heavy fuel prices by 5–8 per cent and diesel fuel prices by approximately 10 per cent. The tax comprised a fiscal component, a carbon component and an energy component, and, unlike all other European examples, did not include exemptions or reductions for any industry sector. In 1995 the basic tax on energy raised revenues of Mk10,200 million and the additional energy/CO_2 tax accounted for an additional Mk2,400 million.[4]

The system was revised again in 1997, partly because of concerns about conflicts with EU legislation, and also following a case brought by Outokumpu Oy, a large mining and metal engineering company. The company bought electricity from Sweden and argued that its imports were discriminated against at the Finnish border because Finland implemented a border tax adjustment (a small import tax) to compensate for the fact that domestically produced electricity was taxed whereas Swedish electricity exports were tax-exempt. The import tax was levied at the *average* rate of electricity taxation in Finland, which was higher than the tax on domestic hydro power, though lower than on other domestically produced electricity. The company argued that the minimum tax rate should have been applied, and the European Court of Justice, overruling the initial opinion from the EU Attorney-General, agreed. The CO_2 tax was therefore modified to tax the output of electricity – i.e. only the energy content, not the carbon inputs – from 1997 on. Rates were increased substantially and differentiated between sectors. Whereas households have to pay the full rate of Mk0.033/kWh, industry and commercial greenhouses pay Mk0.0145, about 40 per cent of the full rate.

The Netherlands

The Netherlands introduced an environmental tax on fuels in 1988 with the specific intention of financing environmental policy initiatives, though since 1992 it has formed part of the general revenue. The level is set to achieve revenue requirements based on consumption in the previous year, and, also since 1992, it is assessed on the energy and the carbon content of the fuel (50:50). The 1996 tax rates were Dfl0.3906/GJ (energy) and Dfl5.16/tCO_2 together roughly equal to a tax rate of $3 per barrel of oil equivalent. Exemptions were granted to district heating and gas-fired electricity generation in order to encourage the market for combined heat and power generation.

---

[4] OECD, *Environmental Taxes in OECD Countries.*

The system was revised in 1996, with the introduction of an additional energy regulatory tax for small consumers. No tax is payable on consumption below a subsistence minimum and above various thresholds, aiming not to damage the competitiveness of industry – it applies to about 40 per cent of non-transport, non-feedstock energy use. The tax on gas is being introduced in three stages, ultimately raising gas prices by 20–25 per cent; electricity prices have risen by 15 per cent in a single step.

With regard to motor fuel taxation, Dutch policy is partly dependent on the German position, as high levels of taxation already provide an incentive for Dutch motorists to drive over the border to fill their tanks. The Netherlands government therefore proposed the differentiation of mineral oil excises regionally, setting lower rates along the German border, but this was not permitted by the European Commission under single market legislation. The government adopted an alternative route, and now pays subsidies of up to £100,000 over three years to filling stations located close to the German border (graduated according to distance from the border), thus compensating for any reductions in profits due to lower prices in Germany.

The revenue from the environmental tax is treated as general government revenue, whereas the revenue from the energy tax is used to reduce income tax and employers' social security contributions. Together, the two taxes should account for about 2.5 per cent of total tax revenue in 1998. The impact of the energy tax on carbon dioxide emissions is projected as 1.5 per cent of total emissions, or 5 per cent of emissions from the affected sectors, by 2000.

Norway

The Norwegian carbon tax was introduced in 1991, starting at a rate of $40.1/tonne CO_2 on petrol; it was also applied to diesel, mineral oil, oil and gas used in North Sea extraction activities (but not onshore gas). It is now applied at levels ranging from $17–55.6/tonne CO_2, and has not been increased in real terms in recent years. It is additional to excise duties, which are equivalent to $239.6/tonne CO_2 for petrol and $176/tonne CO_2 for diesel oil – though for fuel oil for industrial and household use, excise duties were reduced to compensate, stabilizing prices over the period 1991–4. For mineral oil, the pulp and paper, and fish meal industries, pay half the standard rate, and air and maritime transport are exempted.[5]

The carbon tax covers about 60 per cent of all Norwegian CO_2 emissions, and in 1994 generated revenue of approximately NKr6 billion (about 0.7 per cent of total tax revenue) for the general budget. The total impact of the tax over the first three years of implementation, 1991–3, is estimated at a 3–4 per cent reduction in carbon dioxide emissions; the effects on fuel prices were increases of 11–17 per cent (fuel oil) and 9–11 per cent (petrol).

Sweden

In 1990, Sweden adopted sweeping fiscal reforms designed to take environmental objectives into account in the tax system. A carbon tax amounting to SKr250/tCO_2 was introduced in the following year and levied on oil, coal, natural gas and petroleum at differentiated rates;[6] fuel use for electricity production was exempted. At the same time the pre-existing energy tax was reduced, but the net effect was still an increase in taxation. For any single company, there was to be a ceiling on the total amount of energy taxes paid, related to the value of the manufactured products, but the system proved administratively complex and vulnerable to evasion.

The system was revised in 1993 after the European Community's failure to adopt its proposed energy/carbon tax. The carbon tax was raised from SKr250/tCO_2 to SKr320/tCO_2, but non-service industry was given a 75 per cent reduction from this base level (apart from the carbon tax levied on transport fuels), and the energy tax for industry and horticulture was reduced to zero. Electricity generation is exempted from the carbon tax.

The carbon tax is automatically adjusted for inflation. In 1996 it stood at SKr370/tCO_2. In mid-1997 the tax on industry was raised to

---

[5] See below, section 5.1, for Norway's short-lived attempt in January 1999 to introduce taxation on aviation fuel.

[6] The tax was also imposed upon domestic air travel – see Chapter 5.

50 per cent of the base level, after evidence of significant growth in industrial energy consumption. Reduced rates are available for energy-intensive industries. In addition to all this, two taxes on sulphur and nitrogen oxide emissions are also applied.

Total tax revenue from the carbon tax amounted to SKr10.3 billion in 1993, 2.5 per cent of total central government revenues, whereas other energy taxes contributed SKr36 billion. The revenue was used, along with other tax changes, to reduce direct taxes on households and corporations. The complexity of the interacting taxes means that assessment of the impact on carbon dioxide emissions is difficult, but substantial changes in the demand for various fuels following the tax changes shows the sensitivity of energy consumption to price changes.

Germany

The German position on energy taxes changed radically following the election of September 1998. The former coalition between the Christian Democrats and the Free Democrats had argued for a higher rate of VAT on energy consumption, applied on an EU-wide basis to avoid competitiveness impacts – but did not succeed in convincing other member states. The new Social Democrat-Green government, however, adopted a very different approach in the coalition agreement of October 1998.

As a first step, the existing mineral oil taxes on petrol and diesel, heating oil and gas were all to be increased, and a new tax applied to electricity, though fossil fuels (and renewable sources) used as inputs to electricity generation were to be exempt, as was energy-intensive industry. Additional incentives were to be created for greater efficiency in electricity generation. This proposal was very similar to the EC's proposed Energy Products Directive, and the German government was to aim to achieve adoption of the Directive during its Presidency in the first half of 1999. It was also to argue for a European initiative to end the exemption of aviation and marine bunker fuels from international taxation (see Chapter 5) and the so-called 'producer privilege' (the exemption from taxation of energy consumption in refineries).

The impact of these tax increases was projected as 4–5 per cent on transport fuels, almost 10 per cent on heating oil, about 7–8 per cent for electricity and about 6–7 per cent for gas. The tax increases were expected to generate about DM12 billion in the first year, which would be used to reduce both employers' and employees' social security contributions, together accounting for 42.3 per cent of gross salary, by 0.8 per cent. Further steps were to be taken once the outcome of the discussions at EU level was known, and the long-term aim was to reduce social security payments to under 40 per cent (using other revenue sources as well). Some of the revenue was also to be used to increase support to low-income households, possibly through increases in housing subsidies.

The first stage of the proposals was implemented on 1 April 1999, and included, in the light of the failure to make progress with EU-level taxation, reduced rates and exemptions for energy-intensive sectors, including agriculture and rail transport. The European Commission initially questioned the exemptions as giving these firms an unfair advantage, but later in April approved them, accepting that the system was very much in line with the Commission's own approach to energy taxation.

UK

As with Germany, a change in government shifted the position of energy taxes in the UK. Prior to the 1997 general election, the Conservative government had opposed the application of energy or carbon taxes to industry. Its proposed removal of the VAT zero-rating for domestic gas and electricity (taken almost entirely for revenue generation, not environmental, purposes) and the application of VAT at 17.5 per cent had been halted at the interim stage (8 per cent), by a defeat in the House of Commons. The government did, however, increase transport fuel prices by 3 per cent (later 5 per cent) a year in real terms through the so-called 'fuel duty escalator'.

The Labour government which took office in May 1997 reduced VAT on domestic energy to 5 per cent, in an attempt to protect low-income households. They also increased the transport fuel duty escalator to 6 per cent a year in real terms (resulting now in some of the highest fuel taxes in Europe) and appointed a commission to investigate the use of economic instruments in reducing energy use in industry. The Marshall Commission, named after its chair, reported in November 1998, and the government broadly accepted its proposals in the March 1999 Budget. The Commission found much to support in the concept of an emissions trading system (see Chapter 6) but believed its implementation in the UK alone was probably unrealistic, certainly in the short term. Marshall therefore opted for an energy tax, applied downstream (as the domestic and transport sectors were specifically excluded from his brief, an upstream tax was not feasible) and possibly varied by type of fuel to tax carbon-intensive fuels more heavily. The government is currently consulting over the details of the proposal, with the aim of introducing it in April 2001. Media speculation suggested that the tax might raise £1–1.5 billion in the first year, with phased increases thereafter. Marshall suggested recycling the revenue to industry in the form of reductions in other taxes and support for energy-efficiency investments, particularly in the energy-intensive sector.

USA

Progress outside the EU has been even less impressive – as typified by the fate of the United States' proposed federal BTU (British Thermal Unit) tax. This was put forward by the new Clinton administration in 1993, primarily for revenue generation purposes, though the environmental benefits were also highlighted. It would have taxed virtually all forms of fossil fuel energy and would have significantly increased fuel prices for all end users, consumers and producers, although the total scale of taxation on energy would still have been lower than that in most European countries. Although it included a number of exemptions, it was a broad-based and inclusive proposal. Ultimately the proposal foundered upon the opposition of business interests, most notably the powerful fossil fuel lobby.

4.2 Energy taxation and international competitiveness

As can be seen from this description of energy and carbon taxes, the impact of carbon and energy taxation on international competitiveness has been a constant concern to policy-makers introducing the taxes. (This is not an issue if the taxation is applied internationally, of course, but the prospects even for taxation at EU level, let alone across any wider group of countries, seem remote. Chapter 5 discusses the area in which international taxation is probably least unlikely, international bunker fuels for aviation and maritime transport.) It seems self-evident, after all, that the imposition of additional costs on firms through carbon or energy taxation (without any offsetting action) will affect negatively their competitive position *vis-à-vis* other firms that do not face the same costs, particularly in overseas markets.

It should be noted at this point, however, that this is not necessarily the case. There are many opportunities for energy efficiency invest-ments available in most industrialized economies which are not taken up for a wide variety of reasons, including market failure, lack of knowledge and mistaken perceptions.

Furthermore, even if the tax in question does not trigger any behavioural response, its impact on total costs is likely to be low, at least at the rates that are generally proposed in the current debate (and have been applied in various countries to date), particularly when compared with other factors affecting price levels such as exchange rate varia-tions, which may be far more substantial than the tax impact. There have been many studies of potential impacts, including, for example:

- A 1991 UK study[7] of a tax of $100/tC gave an impact of 1.6 per cent increase in costs for all industry. The four sectors worst af-fected were non-ferrous metals, non-metallic minerals, iron and steel, and chemicals, all falling into a 3.8–4.5 per cent range for cost rises.
- A 1997 OECD study[8] of the same level of tax applied across all Annex I countries showed a lower impact in the UK, with the same

---

[7] J. Pezzey, *Impacts of Greenhouse Gas Control Strategies on UK Competitiveness: A Survey and Exploration of the Issues,* Report to the UK Department of Trade and Industry, 1992.

[8] Richard Baron, *Annex I Expert Group on the UNFCCC: Policies and Measures for Common Action – Economic/Fiscal Instruments: Competitiveness Issues Related to Carbon/Energy Taxation* (Bonn: UNFCCC, 1997).

four sectors coming in between 1.2 per cent and 3.6 per cent of costs. The average for energy-intensive industries was 1.2 per cent in Japan, 1.6 per cent in the UK and Germany, 2.8 per cent in the US and 5.2 per cent in Australia. The report concluded that 'cost increases from carbon/energy taxation ought to be compared with other factors affecting price levels such as exchange rate variations and cyclical variations in stocks ... changes in the international markets for energy-intensive products may well dwarf the price effects of a tax'.

This finding, that energy or carbon taxation is unlikely to impact heavily any particular sector of industry, is in line with the results of more general work on the impacts of environmental regulation on industrial costs, competitiveness and investment decisions.

Nevertheless, it is clear that many participants in the debate behave as though they believe precisely the opposite. Political realities are that (a) the introduction of new taxes is never likely to be popular; and (b) that industry is generally a very powerful lobby. It was primarily opposition from industry that sank the US proposal for a BTU tax, and helped defeat the European Commission's proposal for a carbon/energy tax, in the early 1990s, and those European countries which have implemented carbon or energy taxation for environmental reasons have almost all given exemptions or reductions to the industrial sector, in general explicitly because of perceived concerns over competitiveness (although in some cases these are accompanied by voluntary agreements with the sector concerned to limit carbon emissions).

Energy-intensive sectors – such as non-ferrous metals, non-metallic minerals, iron and steel and chemicals – are a particular concern because of their high rates of energy consumption and because (as a consequence) they tend already to be relatively energy-efficient compared to many other industrial sectors. They are therefore more sensitive to the impacts of energy or carbon taxation. If the impact of the tax is severe enough to trigger industrial migration,[9] say to a non-Annex I

---

[9] Considering the impact of environmental costs on international competitiveness as a whole, the evidence for industrial migration is scant, but it is not entirely lacking.

country without limits on carbon emissions, then the tax may in practice actually fail to limit global emissions. In addition, if the pattern of production of energy-intensive products shifts to favour the development of the industry in question in developing countries, then the generally poor standards and enforcement of environmental regulations there, and the prevalence of subsidies for fossil fuel prices, may result in a global increase in carbon (and other) emissions.

It may therefore be desirable for a number of reasons to introduce policy measures that offset any real or perceived negative competitiveness impacts from the carbon or energy tax (in the absence of international coordination in taxation). In principle, there are three broad possibilities:

1. Exemptions from the tax, or rebates, for industry or particular sectors;
2. Recycling of revenue;
3. Border tax adjustments.

Exemptions

In practice this is the main route which countries have tended to follow, building in exemptions or rebates for industry as a whole or for particular sectors, for example, energy-intensive and/or export-oriented industry. Yet there are many reasons to avoid exemptions. Clearly, they reduce the overall effectiveness of the tax, require a higher rate of tax for the non-exempt sectors and increase the social costs of achieving a given level of emissions reductions. Exemptions reduce the incentive to develop more efficient processes and to substitute away from carbon-intensive production, and also generate administrative complexity which in turn encourages tax evasion. They also reduce the revenue raised by such taxes – one estimate suggested that exempting the most energy intensive 20 per cent of US industry from a carbon tax would reduce the revenue generated by almost half.[10] Finally, complex tax

---

[10] J. A. Hoerner and F. Muller, *Carbon Taxes for Climate Protection in a Competitive World* (Bern: Swiss Federal Office for International Economic Affairs, 1996).

policies that provide exemptions, rebates or reductions to the most polluting industries engender considerable opposition amongst environmental groups and the public in general.

Revenue recycling

Many countries have adopted the route of recycling the revenue raised
from the tax back into the economy in some form (as well as using
exemptions and rebates). There are many options, of which the most
straightforward is reducing other taxes, such as business or corporation tax, or employment or labour tax. Alternatively, the tax revenue
can simply be handed back on the basis, say, of share of production,
which still establishes an incentive to reduce energy use or carbon
emissions; this system can be operated at an economy-wide or sector-
wide level. Revenue from the Swedish NOx (nitrogen oxides) charge,
for example, is refunded to the plants that pay it in proportion to their
relative energy efficiency. Finally, it is also possible to recycle the revenue in the form of grants for particular investments, say in energy-
efficiency measures or research and development. Whatever the form of
revenue recycling chosen, it will obviously have a greater effect on energy use or emissions if it is more precisely directed towards behavioural
change.

Economic modelling of such a tax shift generally shows positive
impacts on the economy as a whole, in terms of economic growth and
competitiveness, though the sectoral impacts of course vary. The 1991
UK study referred to earlier showed a lower impact on the worst-affected
sector, of no more than 2.9 per cent of costs, when the carbon tax revenue
was recycled into subsidies per unit of production. Whereas the four
energy-intensive sectors, which accounted for 16 per cent of UK exports,
were still relatively disadvantaged, sectors which accounted for 55 per
cent of exports were relatively advantaged.

Revenue recycling is clearly a more attractive option, from an environmental point of view, than exemptions. It is not without its problems, however; the incidence of different taxes is always different
(energy-intensive industry, for example, tends to be capital- but not
labour-intensive, and would therefore still be affected more heavily),

and credits or grants for investments may simply result in paying industry to make investments it would have made anyway, or to make excessive investment ('gold-plating').

4.3 Border tax adjustments

Given the drawbacks of the other two policy options, there may therefore be an argument for the use of the third type of compensatory or protective measure: border tax adjustments (BTAs). These are defined as:

> Any fiscal measures which put into effect, in whole or in part, the destination principle (i.e. which enable exported products to be relieved of some or all of the tax charged in the exporting country in respect of similar domestic products sold to consumers on the home market and which enable imported products sold to consumers to be charged with some or all of the tax charged in the importing country in respect of similar domestic products).

This definition, drawn up by the OECD, was accepted by a GATT Working Party on Border Tax Adjustments, which reported in December 1970. The application of BTAs enables a country to tax its domestic industry for internal purposes while preserving its competitiveness internationally by allowing its exports to compete untaxed in international markets, and domestically by taxing imports to the same degree.

Can this be achieved in reality? Economists have argued for BTAs since David Ricardo, in 1824, first stated the 'destination principle', i.e. that goods should be taxed in their country of consumption. The second Act of the new United States Congress, in 1789, wrote this into US law by establishing duties on goods imported into the US and providing for the drawback of duties when those goods were re-exported. And there are many examples around us every day. Petrol, cigarettes and alcohol, for example, are subject to the same excise duties in the UK regardless of where they are produced.

When considering BTAs for carbon or energy taxes, however, the picture is more complicated. The main issue arises, of course, from the impact of the taxation on the manufacturing and processing industries and their products, particularly for energy-intensive sectors. Can the BTA be applied to products on the basis of the tax paid on the inputs of energy or carbon *during* production – i.e. on the *process* rather than the product? There are two issues to consider:

- The practicalities of the tax adjustment process – dealt with in the remainder of this section.
- The interrelationship of the BTAs with the multilateral trading system – considered in section 4.4.

Border tax adjustments: practicalities

Although border tax adjustments applied to products are commonplace, BTAs applied on the basis of processes are far more rare. They have been used, however, in the US in two important instances of environmental excise taxes; the Superfund Chemical Excises (Superfund tax) and the Ozone-Depleting Chemicals (ODC) tax.[11] It is possible to draw important lessons from their application for potential BTAs applied in the case of future carbon and/or energy taxes.

(It is also worth noting the two taxes' treatment under the MTS. The ODC tax has never been challenged under the GATT, whereas the Superfund tax was, in 1987; it was found to be GATT-compatible (see below).)

The Superfund tax

The United States Superfund Amendments and Reauthorization Act of 1986 created a system of taxes to fund the clean-up of toxic waste disposal sites, including a petroleum products excise tax, a corporate income tax surcharge and a system of excise taxes on specified chemicals and derivatives. The chemical excise tax applied to the sale or use of the specified chemicals in the US; it was paid by the manufacturer or

---

[11] The descriptions and analysis in this section draws heavily on J. Andrew Hoerner and Frank Muller, 'Carbon Taxes for Climate Protection in a Competitive World' (Swiss Federal Office for International Economic Affairs, 1996); and J. Andrew Hoerner, 'The Role of Border Tax Adjustments in Environmental Taxation: Theory and US Experience', paper delivered at Institute for Environmental Studies' International Workshop on Market-Based Instruments and International Trade (Amsterdam, March 1998).

by the importer, and any tax already paid on exports was rebated. The tax rate varied by chemical, but at the highest was just under $5 per ton, a very modest rate.

These border adjustments applied to the chemicals listed in the relevant legislation and also to other chemicals manufactured using taxed chemicals as feedstock. These derivatives were not themselves subject to the excise taxes, but imports of them were subject to the tax, and exports were similarly rebated, as long as taxable chemicals constituted at least 50 per cent of the chemicals used to produce the final substance, by weight or value.

The BTA was imposed on the importer at the point of first sale or use. If the importer provided detailed information on the taxable chemicals actually used in the manufacture of the imported substance, the tax was based on the amount of the tax that would have been paid if the substance had been manufactured in the US. If this information was not supplied, the tax was applied according to US Treasury regulations which listed, for each substance, the amount of taxed chemicals used in its manufacture under the predominant method employed in the US. If a substance was not listed in the regulations, a flat rate of 5 per cent of the value of the import was applied. Exporters of taxable substances were granted credits or refunds for the taxes already paid.

So far, this has described a fairly straightforward BTA applied to a product. The important point to note, however, is that the tax was calculated according to the amount of chemicals used in the manufacturing process; it was not necessary for all of the atoms contained in the taxable chemical to be physically incorporated into the final substance, and the tax rate was not adjusted if only a portion of the original chemicals were actually present at the end. Thus it was a true *process*-based BTA.

As considered further below, in 1987 a GATT dispute panel found for the US in a dispute with Canada, Mexico and EU over the application of these BTAs. It decided that for the purposes of GATT Article III, the BTA did not treat imports differently from like products produced in the US, whether the tax was calculated according to the actual data on manufacturing or on the predominant method in use in the US. It did, however, find against the 5 per cent tax for unlisted substances, on the grounds that this imposed a higher tax in imports than on like domestic products.

The ODC tax

In order to accomplish the phase-out of ozone-depleting substances such as CFCs under the terms of the 1987 Montreal Protocol, the US decided to impose a system of excise taxes as well as production allowances for their manufacturers. The tax was applied to the chemicals at rates generally proportional to their ozone-depleting potential, and increased year by year; a floor stocks tax was also introduced to ensure that stockpiles of substances produced in one year could not be sold at a lower price in future years.

As with the Superfund tax, importers were liable for taxes on imported ODCs at the point of first sale or use, at rates equal to the domestic taxes, and exporters (or manufacturers) were eligible for rebates. Unlike the Superfund tax, the ODC excise tax was set at a relatively high rate; in 1994–5, for example, the taxed price of CFC-11 and CFC-12 (the most commonly used CFCs) was roughly triple the untaxed price. Coupled with a high demand for CFCs as coolants in vehicle air conditioners, this fuelled the growth of substantial illegal imports of the substances into the US – a problem which still remains, although now at a somewhat smaller scale.[12]

BTAs also apply to imports of all products containing or produced with ODCs, subject to a *de minimis* floor for trivial amounts of such products, though this does not apply to refrigeration or air-conditioning equipment, aerosols or foams or electronic equipment – which covers most of the main uses of ODCs. Treasury regulations have set the *de minimis* level at 0.1 per cent of the cost to the importer of acquiring the product, which in fact has covered all of the products manufactured with but not containing ODCs outside the list of excluded products.

---

[12] For a fuller treatment of this subject, see Duncan Brack, *International Trade and the Montreal Protocol* (London: RIIA/Earthscan, 1996); and Duncan Brack, 'The Growth and Control of Illegal Trade in Ozone-Depleting Substances', paper delivered at the 1997 Taipei International Conference on Ozone Layer Protection (December 1997).

Imports of products containing ODCs (for example, refrigerators), manufactured with ODCs (for example, electronic components, which are often cleaned with ODC-containing solvents), or chemical mixtures containing ODCs are subject to tax at the rate which would have been paid on the chemicals used in their manufacture if they had been made in the US. As with the Superfund tax, the ODC tax is based on the actual consumption of ODCs, if reported, or on a determination of the amounts used in the predominant production methods in the US, if not reported. Unlike the Superfund tax, there is no export rebate for products containing or made with ODCs. Once again, however, these BTAs are both product and process-related.

Lessons from the US experience

'The US experience', wrote one observer in 1998, 'especially with the ODC tax, established the importance of BTAs to achieving the benefits of environmental taxation. As a result of the BTA system, the domestic ODC industry was protected from foreign predation while an orderly phase-out of ODCs was achieved ... the ODC tax was high enough that, without the BTAs, the domestic industry would have been rapidly extinguished by foreign imports, with no resulting benefit to the global environment. Given this market reality, the political reality is that the US Congress would never have enacted the ODC tax without BTAs'.[13]

While it can be questioned whether the US actually needed the ODC tax to phase out the use of the chemicals – other countries, including the EU, have achieved a faster speed of phase-out without using such taxes[14] – it is clearly their government's right to decide the matter. Given the domestic reduction of ODC consumption in other manufacturing (chiefly EU) countries, and the recent substantial growth in manufacturing capacity in developing countries (mainly India and China),

---

[13] Hoerner, 'The Role of Border Tax Adjustments in Environmental Experience', p. 14.

[14] Though it should be remembered that with 90% of its vehicle fleet equipped with air conditioners (which need regular servicing and refilling with coolants), the US faced a far more dispersed market for ODCs than did European countries (where only about 10% of vehicles tend to be fitted with air conditioners), thus making the use of a tax, alongside regulations, rather more attractive.

who face no controls on production until mid-1999, the fear of foreign import penetration was a real one.

A number of lessons can be drawn from the experience of BTAs under the Superfund and ODC taxes:[15]

- A tax on embodied inputs can be administered; the absence of the original (taxable) chemicals in the final product is not a bar to the application of import taxes or export rebates.
- BTAs should be avoided where the tax is a trivial proportion of the price; the 50 per cent floor for the Superfund tax, and the *de minimis* rule for non-listed products for the ODC tax, helped to avoid the substantial administrative burden of calculating extremely small amounts of taxes with very little environmental benefit. This could have been extended; the value of ODCs used in cleaning electronic components, for example, is very small indeed.
- If the tax reaches a significant proportion of the final price, there will be evasion, including the growth of illegal trade. This is not a problem which is unique to BTAs, however; it stems from the relative prices and availabilities of the controlled products and their alternatives. The EU, without an ODC tax, has suffered quite significant volumes of illegal imports. However, the use of taxes and BTAs is clearly likely to exacerbate such problems.

Application of process-based BTAs to carbon/energy taxes

The application of the US experience with the Superfund and ODC tax BTAs to carbon or energy taxes is not completely straightforward. The number of products that would be covered is of course much wider, though the use of a *de minimis* floor would rule out a significant proportion. During the US debates over the BTU tax legislation introduced by the new Clinton administration in 1993, it was proposed that BTAs should be applied to all goods for which the cost of energy would exceed 2 per cent of the cost of production. Since the tax would have raised average energy costs by only 4–6 per cent, this would have ap-

---

[15] Hoerner, 'The Role of Border Tax Adjustments in Environmental Experience', pp. 15–16.

plied BTAs to a very wide range of products, where the value of the tax was only about 0.1 per cent of their value. By contrast, if the 2 per cent floor was applied on the cost of the energy *tax* rather than the cost of *energy*, it would have ruled out all by a tiny handful of energy-intensive materials.

As with any process-based trade measure, acquiring the relevant information is crucial. If the data is provided by the importer (and can be verified), this need cause no problem, but mechanisms must be devised to cope in the absence of the data. The US use of 'predominant method of manufacture' comparisons would be difficult to apply in the case of carbon or energy taxes, given the wide range of manufacturing and processing techniques in use around the world, and the very different fuel mixes used by different countries. Once again, however, the problem becomes much smaller if the range of products subject to BTAs is relatively small; for energy-intensive products such as aluminium, relatively good data are probably available on manufacturing products, and the average fuel mix of different countries is known with some accuracy.

The next question to ask, therefore, is whether BTAs are compatible with the multilateral trading system.

4.4 Border tax adjustment and the multilateral trading system[16]

Taxes imposed on imports (or rebated on exports) are obviously barriers to trade, so do fall within the scope of the multilateral trading system. The question therefore becomes: do the provisions of the MTS permit BTAs for energy and carbon taxes? The problem – and this is the main element causing confusion in this debate – is that there is no clear answer.

Many crucial terms, such as 'like product', which are used in the GATT, are nowhere defined. This is not unusual for treaties, but in other regimes such as multilateral environmental agreements, for ex-

---

[16] Much of the material in this section is drawn from Richard A. Westin: *Environmental Tax Initiatives and Multilateral Trade Agreements: Dangerous Collisions* (The Hague/London/Boston: Kluwer Law International, 1997).

ample, there is a clear procedure for agreeing definitions of terms: the conference or meeting of the parties takes a decision. In contrast, the GATT and other WTO agreements evolve through a case law-type approach, where meanings and interpretations of terms can be deduced through the decisions of dispute panels and the Appellate Body – which, themselves, of course, tend to evolve over time. The problem here is that there has never been a GATT or WTO dispute case involving energy or carbon taxes. We therefore have to infer the answer to the question from the text of GATT and other WTO agreements, from dispute panel rulings in other cases (such as those dealing with other taxes, or with the definition of relevant terms), and, in this case, from the conclusions of the 1970 GATT Working Party on BTAs. It should be stressed, however, that there will be no clear answer to the question until there is an apposite panel ruling, or unless the GATT text is renegotiated in some way to deal with the issue (which is highly unlikely).

There are two cases to examine:

1. The application of energy or carbon taxes directly to imports (and rebated on exports) of energy *sources*, such as fossil fuels.
2. The application of BTAs to products on the basis of the taxes paid during their production processes.

Border tax adjustments: energy sources

The first case (energy sources, such as fossil fuels, themselves), as one would expect, is relatively straightforward. The 1970 Working Party distinguished between direct taxes, such as those on wages, profits, interests, rents, royalties, and all other forms of income, and taxes on the ownership of real property, and indirect taxes such as sales, excise, turnover, value-added, franchise, stamp, transfer, inventory and equipment taxes. It accepted that indirect taxes alone were eligible for tax adjustment at the border, and this conclusion has not been challenged since.

It is important to bear in mind the general GATT principles of nondiscrimination. The tax in question must therefore apply both to imports and to domestic production (i.e. we are not considering import duties or tariffs), and it must be applied to imported and domestic 'like products' equally. In fact, two requirements are stipulated in Article III of the GATT: that a BTA should not discriminate between like products; and that it should not 'afford protection to domestic production'.

The meaning of the term 'like product' is highly controversial – a subject to which we will return later – but in this context it causes no real problem. As long as the tax adjustment does not discriminate against imports, it is acceptable under the GATT. It is also worth noting in passing that the *purpose* of the tax, whether it is environmental protection, revenue generation or anything else, is not relevant to the GATT. This conclusion was explicitly stated in the findings of the Superfund case of 1987 (see section 4.3), where the dispute panel found that the US was allowed to tax imports of particular chemicals on the same basis as domestically-produced equivalents were taxed, even though the ostensible purpose of the tax was to prevent pollution from the manufacture of the chemicals in the US. If the polluter-pays principle had been followed, the imports would not have been taxed, since the pollution occurred in the country of manufacture; but the only important factor from the GATT point of view is whether the tax adjustment is protective of domestic industry in practice.

This analysis has so far referred to imports, but it can also be applied to exports. The rebate of indirect taxes on exports is in fact explicitly permitted under the WTO Agreement on Subsidies and Countervailing Measures (SCM Agreement; see further in section 4.5) since, of course, an export rebate is in practice equivalent to a subsidy. Under the SCM Agreement, such a rebate is not countervailable if it is applied to an indirect (and not a direct) tax and if the rebate is not bigger than the size of the domestic tax.

Border tax adjustments: processes

The main issue for BTAs for carbon or energy taxes arises, of course, from the impact of the taxation on the manufacturing and processing industries and their products, particularly for energy-intensive sectors. Can the BTA be applied to products on the basis of the tax paid on the inputs of energy or carbon *during* production?

The 1970 GATT Working Party considered this question but failed to reach a conclusion. It noted that 'there was a divergence of views with regard to the eligibility for adjustment of certain categories of tax', such as the *taxes occultes*, which encompass consumption taxes on capital equipment, auxiliary materials and services used in the transportation and production of other taxable goods, as well as taxes on advertising, energy, machinery and transport. The Working Party did not investigate the matter; it felt that 'while this area of taxation was unclear, its importance – as indicated by the scarcity of complaints reported in connection with adjustments of *taxes occultes* – was not such as to justify further examination'.[17] A fair enough conclusion in 1970, but not now.

Imports

Examining the text of the GATT, the indications are that BTA is allowable on imports physically incorporated into the final product. Article II:2(a) stipulates that border tax adjustment can be made with respect to 'a charge equivalent to an internal tax imposed consistently with the provisions of paragraph 2 of Article III [footnote omitted] in respect of the like imported product *or in respect of an article from which the imported product has been manufactured or produced in whole or in part*' [emphasis added]. During the original negotiations on the GATT, it was agreed that the word 'equivalent' meant, 'for example, if a [charge] is imposed on perfume because it contains alcohol, the [charge] to be imposed must take into consideration the value of the alcohol and not the value of the perfume, that is to say the value of the content and not the value of the whole'.[18] This is reinforced by the findings of the Superfund case, in which the US tax was imposed on imports from Europe because they were manufactured from chemicals that would have been subject to an excise tax in the US.

This argument, however, refers to inputs physically incorporated into the final product. Can this apply to energy consumed, or to carbon emitted, during production? There are no precedents in any part of the

---

[17] BISD 18S/97, para. 15.
[18] EPCT/TAC/PV/26, p. 21, referred to in Analytical Index, Guide to GATT Law and Practice, vol. 1, p. 86.

GATT or associated agreements; this dimension of the question would be entirely up to a dispute panel to settle.

Exports

The question of exports is more complicated; as noted above, export subsidies (in this case, tax rebates on exports) are covered by the SCM Agreement. This specifically allows the rebating of prior-stage cumulative indirect taxes on goods or services used in the production of exported products – but only to the extent that the goods and services in question are 'consumed in the production process' and that the taxes exempted are not in excess of such taxes on goods and services used in the production of like products for domestic consumption (i.e. exports are not treated more favourably than domestic production). The infamous footnote 61 to this paragraph of the SCM Agreement adds the definition that 'inputs consumed in the production process are inputs physically incorporated, energy, fuels and oil used in the production process and catalysts which are consumed in the course of their use to obtain the exported product'.

In other words, taxes on the items listed in footnote 61 – including 'energy, fuels and oil used in the production process' – *can* be adjustable at the border, at least for exports. Unlike the situation for imports, this would appear to permit BTAs for energy or carbon taxes based on processes.

However, this entire paragraph relates to 'prior-stage cumulative indirect taxes', which are further defined in the Agreement as follows:

- 'Prior-stage indirect taxes' are those levied on goods or services used directly or indirectly in making the product.
- 'Cumulative' indirect taxes are multi-staged taxes levied where there is no mechanism for subsequent crediting of the tax if the goods or services subject to tax at one stage of production are used in a succeeding stage of production.

The earlier term used, *taxes occultes* – such as excise duties – are arguably *not* 'cumulative' taxes because the energy or carbon is taxed only once, and the same input is never used in a succeeding stage of taxation, as with a cumulative tax. The archetypal prior-stage cumulative indirect tax is a cascade tax, which imposes an *ad valorem* tax on all transfers of goods, including those used as inputs to manufacturing. Cascade taxes cumulate: inputs are taxed, and the outputs are taxed as well. Cascade taxes used to be quite common in Europe, but have now been entirely replaced by VAT. They are still used, however, in a number of developing countries, including India.

So where does that leave us? *Probably*, the definition in footnote 61 – which would appear to allow the BTAs we are considering – does *not* apply to carbon or energy taxes. There are three supporting reasons for this conclusion:

1. The 1979 Subsidies Code (which the SCM Agreement replaced) referred to 'goods that are physically incorporated in the exported product'. The signatories of the Code had defined these as 'such inputs [that] are used in the production process and are physically present in the product exported. The signatories note that an input need not be present in the final product in the same form in which it entered the production process'.[19] It seems highly unlikely that the 1994 SCM Agreement really intended to *widen* the scope for BTAs, a step which would be entirely contrary to the general evolution of the multilateral trading system.

2. The possibility of a widening was noted during the Uruguay Round negotiations with some concern. A letter from a USTR official at the time indicated that the new language in the SCM Agreement was the object of an informal agreement among developed countries whereby 'it was proposed to address a specific and very narrow issue involving certain energy-intensive exports from a limited number of countries. It was never intended to fundamentally expand the right of countries to apply border adjustment for a broad range of taxes on energy, especially in the developed world ... . We discussed the matter with other developed countries involved in the Subsidies Code negotiations. We are satisfied that they share our views on the

---

[19] Doc. SCM/68, para. 4.

purpose of the text as drafted and the importance of careful international examination before any broader policy conclusions should be drawn regarding border adjustments and energy taxes'.[20]

3. Finally, and more broadly, the debate over the eligibility of BTAs for carbon or energy taxes for processes relates directly to the ongoing controversy over the meaning of a 'like product'. As discussed in Chapter 1, the GATT's 'like product' provisions were drawn up to outlaw discrimination on the basis of the national origin of the product in question. GATT and WTO dispute panels have applied them, however, in environmental cases to rule against discrimination against products on the basis of the way in which they are produced. This was the issue that underlay the well-known tuna-dolphin dispute of 1991, and many others; dispute panels have been entirely consistent in their findings in this respect, and to allow BTAs in this case would be to run directly against this trend. Having said that, the Appellate Body findings in the 1998 shrimp-turtle case suggested that process-based trade measures might be acceptable if applied in a non-arbitrary way, so this conclusion is not so firm as it would have been before the case concluded.

To conclude this long and rather Byzantine exploration of the details of various GATT texts, it would appear that BTAs relating to production processes are only allowable if they are applied to inputs that are physically incorporated. They appear *not* to be allowable if the input is not present in the final product – which is the case for energy consumed and carbon emitted during production. As above, however, this is not a definite conclusion, and it would have to be tested by a dispute panel before one could be certain.

The saving clause

This is not, however, quite the end of the argument. As explained in Chapter One, the GATT does permit certain unilateral trade restric-

---

[20] Letter from D. Phillips, Assistant USTR for Industry, to A. Katz, President US Council for International Business, referred to in *Inside US Trade*, 28 January 1994.

tions in the pursuit of environmental protection under particular circumstances, through the provisions of Article XX, the 'General Exceptions' clause. A country applying BTAs for energy or carbon taxes
relating to processes could therefore appeal to this clause to 'save' the
action from the problem of inconsistency with other sections of the
GATT.

Once again, we have no experience of how a panel would rule if this
approach were attempted in the case of BTAs. There *is*, however, experience of panels' interpretations of the applicability of Article XX in
other dispute cases. The key arguments revolve around the definition
of 'necessary' (XX(b)) and 'relating to the conservation of natural resources' (XX(g)). Both terms arguably apply to a carbon or energy *tax*,
but of course it is not the tax that is at dispute, but the tax *adjustment* at
the border. Following earlier panel rulings, it is quite likely that a dispute panel would rule that the BTA was *not* necessary under the terms
of Article XX(b), because the tax adjustment is not necessary to the limiting of energy use or carbon emissions. Similarly, on Article XX(g),
earlier panels have interpreted the words 'relating to' as meaning 'primarily aimed at', and it seems quite possible that a panel would decide
that the tax *adjustment* was not primarily aimed at reducing carbon
emissions.

Even if the panel were to conclude that the BTA did qualify under
either paragraph (b) or paragraph (g), it would still have to satisfy the
terms of the headnote to Article XX, i.e. not be 'arbitrary or unjustifiable discrimination'. This may depend on the design of the tax; the
more sophisticated the details – i.e. the more precisely it is applied to
products on the basis of the exact amount of energy consumed, or the
exact quantity of carbon emitted, during production (which, of course,
multiplies the practical difficulties of application enormously) – the
more it could be argued to be *not* 'arbitrary or unjustifiable discrimination' (though the complexity of the administrative processes might
then in practice lead to arbitrary treatment). But it is quite likely that a
panel *would* decide that the BTA was discriminatory because, after all,
the main purpose of the *adjustment* is not to mitigate climate change
but to protect domestic industry from the actual or perceived competitiveness impacts of the tax.

Conclusion: are BTAs allowable?

The likelihood is, therefore, that even if the 'saving clause' of Article XX were to be cited, a WTO dispute panel would find that BTAs for carbon or energy taxes related to processes are not permissible. The point must be repeated, however, that this is not proven until a panel actually reports. The WTO's Committee on Trade and Environment has in fact been discussing the issue of BTAs in general since it was established in 1995, without reaching any conclusion (a common theme for all its discussions).

This conclusion is not particularly surprising. The MTS has in practice proved to be a highly effective international regime, genuinely multilateral in scope, and providing powerful safeguards against protectionism – and although trade liberalization may cause problems for environmental quality, protectionism usually causes far more. Some of the trade-environment cases brought to GATT dispute panels – such as the tuna-dolphin and CAFE disputes – have in fact shown that the trade barriers in question were at least partly protectionist, rather than primarily environmental, in intent.

Some trade barriers, however, clearly are of benefit to the environment, and there are several genuine reasons why it could be argued that the current operation of the multilateral trading system may need to be reformed to permit the more effective protection of the environment. Trade restrictions built into multilateral environmental agreements is one example, and the general prohibition of trade measures based on processes is another. There is, therefore, growing pressure to adjust the way the system operates, possibly through amendment of the GATT.

If BTAs for carbon or energy taxes are genuinely desirable, the current GATT obstacles should not, therefore, be regarded as insuperable – and, given the WTO's general antipathy to unilateral action, it may help if they could be agreed as part of the Kyoto Protocol process. The key question should therefore be: could BTAs be effective in helping to mitigate climate change? The experience of the process-based BTAs described above in section 4.3 suggests that they might be.

Border tax adjustments have tended to be ignored in most countries, other than the US, in the debate around environmental taxation and its

real or perceived impacts on international competitiveness. Given the
major drawbacks of exemptions, and the limited applicability of tax
recycling, however, it deserves far more serious treatment as a mechanism to speed the introduction of carbon or energy taxes in the efforts
to mitigate climate change.

4.5 Subsidies

The final issue to be considered under the question of energy pricing
and trade is the topic of subsidies. These are common in the energy
sector. Examples include:[21]

- Direct subsidies.
- Tax concessions or tax exemptions.
- Low-cost long-term land concessions for energy exploration or
  production activity.
- Government absorption of different risks associated with explora-
  tion or production (such as liability waivers).
- Energy infrastructure subsidies (such as low-cost power transmis-
  sion lines, low-cost land concessions rights and petroleum import
  or export facilities).
- Provision of free accident insurance.
- The provisions of loan guarantees.
- Grants or tax incentives to develop energy-related technologies.
- Transfers to upgrade either commercial or household energy sources.
- Grants or tax incentives to lower operating costs in various energy-
  intensive commercial production activities.
- Transfers to lower household heating bills.

In some cases, subsidies can be provided for environmentally beneficial purposes – for instance in the support of renewable energy generation or energy efficiency investments. In most cases, however, subsidies
increase the use of fossil fuel energy beyond what it would otherwise be,
and thereby contribute to raising greenhouse gas emissions.

---

[21] 'Environmental Benefits of Removing Trade Restrictions and Distortions', note prepared
by the WTO Secretariat, 1998.

Annual energy subsidies in developed countries is estimated at in the vicinity of $70–80 billion[22] In eastern and central Europe electricity subsidies are $34–39 billion a year, though overall energy subsidies in this region have been falling sharply.[23] For developing countries, overall energy subsidies are probably higher than $150 billion per year, of which electricity consumption accounts for $100 billion. Electricity prices in developing countries tend to be less than half of those in developed countries, and in most cases do not cover the long run marginal cost of generation.[24] Other important subsidies in developing countries are directed to reduce kerosene prices (an important energy source for many low-income households) and transport fuel costs.

In general, however, the level of subsidies for fossil fuels is currently falling. The best example is the European coal industry, where subsidies in one form or another have declined substantially; from $16.5 billion in 1989 to $8.1 billion in 1995. According to the World Bank, during the 1990s total fossil fuel subsidies in 14 selected developing countries declined by more than 45 per cent in the face of trade liberalization and domestic market reforms. In China for example, coal subsidies were reduced from 37 per cent in 1984 to 29 per cent in 1995, and petroleum subsidies from 55 per cent in 1990 to 2 per cent in 1995. This trend is evident in India, Mexico, South Africa, Saudi Arabia and Brazil, where fuel subsidies have likewise been reduced significantly in recent years.

Coal is the main destination of subsidies for fossil fuel production and consumption. These take many forms, including market price support, which guarantees a minimum price level for the producer, deficiency payments to producers for sales below the production costs, direct support to research and development[25] and requirements on

---

[22] A. de Moor, *Subsidizing Unsustainable Development* (Amsterdam: Institute for Research and Public Expenditure, 1997).

[23] B. Larsen and A. Shah, 'World Fossil Fuel Subsidies and Global Carbon Emissions', *World Development Report* (Washington: World Bank, 1992).

[24] World Bank, *Expanding the Measure of Wealth: Indicators of Environmentally Sustainable Development* (Washington: World Bank, 1997).

[25] Direct support measures and support to research and development initiatives have been substantially biased in favour of coal and nuclear power. Ruijgroh and Oosterhuis (1995) estimate that support to the nuclear and fossil fuel sectors constituted 75% of total energy sector research and development expenditure within the EU over the period 1990 to 1995.

users, such as electricity generators, to purchase coal. Germany, for example, has provided significant support for its domestic coal industry, amounting in 1990 to $90,200 per miner – several times a miner's annual wage.[26] In addition to these price supports, German electricity generators were also obliged to purchase 87 per cent of their coal from local coal mines during the period 1992–5 at a substantial premium on the world market price.[27] Table 4.2 sets out overall levels of coal subsidies in selected OECD countries in 1993.

Table 4.2: Estimates of producer subsidy equivalents (PSEs) for coal in selected OECD countries, 1993

Country	PSE per tonne coal ($/tce)	Total PSE ($million)	Subsidized production (MTCE)
France	43	428	10.0
Germany	109	6,688	61.5
Japan	161	1,034	6.4
Spain	84	856	10.2
Turkey	143	416	2.9
United Kingdom	15	873	57.4

Source: From DRI, 'Effects of Phasing Out Coal Subsidies in OECD Countries' OECD, *Reforming Energy and Transport Subsidies: Environmental and Economic Implications* (Paris: OECD/IEA, 1997).

Note: PSE is calculated as the subsidy needed to make coal production competitive in an unregulated market.

These various forms of support encourage the overuse of inputs and resources, as well as establishing disincentives against the development of alternative technologies which may be cheaper and more efficient (and less environmentally harmful – for example, combined-cycle gas turbines). They may discriminate against cheaper imports, thereby distorting patterns of trade.

---

[26] K. Anderson, 'The Political Economy of Coal Subsidies in Western Europe', *Energy Policy*, 23:6 (1995), pp. 485–96.

[27] K. Anderson and W. J. McKibbin, 'Reducing Coal Subsidies and Trade Barriers: Their Contribution to Greenhouse Gas Abatement', Seminar Paper 97–107 (Adelaide: Centre for International Economic Studies, 1997).

As indicated above, however, in recent years coal subsidies have been scaled down. Germany has committed itself to significant reductions in coal producer support, falling from approximately DM9.25 billion in 1998 to DM5.5 billion in 2005. In this respect Germany is following the lead of countries such as the United Kingdom, France, Belgium and Japan, each of which have significantly reduced the level of support to domestic coal production since the 1980s. In the United Kingdom only limited price protection remains for what has become, since 1994, a privatized industry; in Belgium the last coal mine ceased production in 1992; and in France domestic coal production is forecast to cease in 2005. This has been the result of a number of factors: constraints upon government expenditure, the general process of deregulation and privatization, and pressures for trade liberalization have probably all been more important than a desire to reduce environmental impacts, though this is steadily gaining in importance, particularly in the context of climate change and the Kyoto Protocol. The process is not likely to be an easy one politically, however, as particular sectors and communities benefiting from the subsidies are always more likely to be more vocal in their defence than those benefiting from their removal are in their abolition (and whereas the costs of subsidy removal are usually concentrated, the benefits are often spread much more widely and felt much less keenly). The political costs of removing support for coal have been demonstrated in several of the countries listed above, notably Germany and the UK, though Britain provides an example of a government that was able largely to face down such opposition.

Environmental impact

The International Energy Agency has commissioned a number of country-specific case studies examining the environmental effects of the removal of such subsidies (Table 4.3). Though considerable variability exists in the estimates, the results are consistent in that they illustrate that the removal of energy sector supports will have a positive effect on reducing not only greenhouse gas emissions, but also those of other air pollutants. The various case studies found that existing energy sector supports total approximately $100 billion per annum (approximately 0.75 per cent of total OECD GDP) and that their removal could reduce greenhouse gas emissions by more than 600 Mt-CO$_2$ equivalent per annum by the year 2010.

Such general conclusions, however, mask the underlying complexity of the issue. It is not just the size, but also the nature of the support

Table 4.3: Summary of results from OECD studies on energy support removal

Study	Nature of support	Size of support	Reduction in CO$_2$ emissions (Mt-CO$_2$eq)
OECD (DRI, 1997)	Coal PSEs in Europe and Japan	5800	10.0
Australia (Naughten et al., 1997)	State procurement planning requirements and barriers to gas and electricity trade	1533	1.1
Italy (Tosato, 1997)	Total net budgetary subsidies and cross-subsidies to the electricity supply industry	10,000	19.2
Norway (Vetlesen and Jensen, 1997)	Barriers to trade	Not quantified	8.0
Russia (Gurvich et al., 1997)	Direct subsidies and price controls for fossil fuels	52,000	336.0
United Kingdom (Michaelis, 1997)	Grants and price supports for coal and nuclear producers and imposition of VAT on electricity below general rates	54,500	0 – 40
United States (Shelby et al., 1997)	Federal energy supply subsidies	15,400	235.0

Source: OECD, *Improving the Environment through Reducing Subsidies, Part II* (Paris: OECD/IEA, 1998).

measures that will determine the effect of their removal on the environment. For example, support to energy producers through tax exemptions or reduced rate loans and limitations on risk and liability, all effectively lower production costs. If, as in the former Soviet bloc countries, this support leads to a reduction in the price at which energy is sold on the domestic market to below that on the world market, the removal of these subsidies will result in higher prices to consumers. Where the primary fuel used is coal, electricity generators will be encouraged to substitute away from coal, and consumers will be encouraged to conserve energy.

If, in contrast, the subsidy includes purchase requirements such as a requirement on electricity generators to purchase domestic coal at a higher price than prevails on the world market (as is, or was, the case in several western European countries such as Germany and the United Kingdom), the removal of such supports may result in lower prices for consumers and thus increased demand for electricity, which could be met by increased coal imports and/or by the expansion of other forms of generation. This has been the experience particularly in the UK, where the outcome of the process of electricity privatization and the introduction of competitive markets has been massive expansion in gas-fired electricity generation and a significant fall in the price of electricity. Whereas the former development has helped ensure that the UK is likely to be one of the very few countries to meet its FCCC target of a stabilization of carbon dioxide emissions at the 1990 level by 2000, the latter effect has helped to undermine incentives for energy conservation investments and contributed to a decline in the average energy efficiency level of households, with worrying long-term effects.

Thus the removal of supports may lead to favourable or unfavourable environmental outcomes, depending upon the nature of the support and the point at which it is imposed on the chain of production. Ironically, the removal of coal sector subsidies in western Europe is forecast to increase coal imports by up to 80Mt per annum – a 15 per cent increase in world coal trade.[28]

---

[28] DRI, 'Effects of Phasing Out Coal Subsidies in OECD Countries' OECD, *Reforming Energy and Transport Subsidies: Environmental and Economic Implications* (Paris: OECD/IEA, 1997).

Subsidies and the multilateral trading system

The gradual evolution of the multilateral trading system has helped to increase pressure for the removal of subsidies, particularly in the area of agriculture. The forthcoming Millennium Round seems likely to focus yet further attention on this area, particularly since the target of earlier rounds – tariff reduction – is now less significant; fisheries may well be added to agriculture as a topic for discussion. The topic of energy subsidies is probably less likely to feature in the discussions, as it is so politically sensitive. In fact, anecdotal evidence suggests that in general countries employ a wide range of subsidies, for all kinds of products, which are strictly WTO-illegal but have not yet been challenged because of the fear of retaliatory challenges. Nevertheless, the evolution of the climate change regime is likely to move the topic up the political agenda, from the point of view both of environmentally damaging subsidies (as described above) and environmentally beneficial subsidies.

The MTS deals with subsidies under the Agreement on Subsidies and Countervailing Measures (SCM Agreement), another of the Uruguay Round agreements, which evolved in this case from the earlier Subsidies Code. The Agreement defines a subsidy as a financial contribution or benefit conferred by a government to domestic industry, including direct transfers, loan guarantees, fiscal incentives such as tax credits, provision of goods and services other than general infrastructure, or direct payments to a funding mechanism. Three categories are listed:

- Prohibited subsidies: that require recipients to meet certain export targets, or to use domestic instead of imported goods. These are clearly trade-distortionary, and can be challenged under the WTO dispute settlement procedure, where they are handled under an accelerated timetable. If they are confirmed as falling within the definition of prohibited, the complaining country can take countervailing measures.
- Actionable subsidies: where the complaining country can show that the subsidy has an adverse effect on its interests (its domestic industry and/or exporters); if no harm can be proved, then the subsidy is permitted.

- Non-actionable subsidies: including non-specific subsidies, particular subsidies for industrial research, assistance to disadvantaged regions, or certain types of assistance for adapting existing facilities to new environmental laws or regulations. These have to meet strict conditions – for example, subsidies to offset increases in production costs of firms adjusting to new environmental regulations must be limited to a one-off payment of no more than 20 per cent of the adaptation costs.

The further development of the SCM Agreement will be helpful to the climate change regime if it increases the pressure to reduce and eliminate subsidies for greenhouse gas-emitting energy production and use. It will be unhelpful if it constrains governments' abilities to provide adjustment assistance to industry – for example, to develop renewable energy sources, or to fit combined heat and power facilities to existing power plants to raise their efficiency – for climate change mitigation purposes. It may be, however, that such subsidies could be applied in the 'non-specific' way defined in the SCM Agreement, i.e. if there are objective and legally enforceable criteria governing eligibility for the amount of the subsidy and if eligibility is automatic for any company meeting the criteria. What is clear is that any discussions around the further development of the SCM Agreement should be informed by an understanding of the value of subsidies in achieving the significant economic restructuring likely to be necessary if the challenge of climate change is successfully met.[29]

4.6 Conclusions

Of all the issues examined in this book, the question of energy pricing policy, and its role in climate change mitigation, is likely to trigger most controversy. Just over the period during which the book was written, several governments have come forward with proposals for new

---

[29] For an excellent, and more comprehensive, treatment of this topic, see Lucas Assunção, 'Trade Rules and Climate Change Policy: Some Issues of Synergy and Conflict', paper delivered to the Royal Institute of International Affairs conference 'Implementing the Kyoto Protocol', June 1999.

or revised energy and/or carbon taxes, generally to be met with hostility from industrial lobbies. The rapid progress of energy market liberalization in some countries, and continued economic strain in many others (including the Asian financial crisis, and IMF-sponsored structural adjustment policies in developing countries) is continuing to exert downward pressure on subsidies for energy production and use. The approach of the WTO Millennium Round is focusing attention on questions of international trade, investment and competitiveness.

Approaching these questions from the objective of rapid action to reduce greenhouse gas emissions gives some clear conclusions. Energy and carbon taxes have a valuable role to play in incorporating environmental externalities – chiefly, climate change – in prices and decision-making, and could usefully be deployed more extensively in more countries. Given the partly real, partly perceived concerns over the impact on international competitiveness, however, some combination of offsetting measures will be necessary. Revenue recycling, either through general reductions in other taxes, and/or through targeted recycling for energy-intensive sectors (either through assistance with energy efficiency improvements or through direct refunds along the lines of the Swedish NOx charge) is hugely preferable to exemptions. In addition, border tax adjustments (probably restricted to a limited range of energy-intensive products and processes) may well prove to be of value, and their practicality should be explored. Subsidies can also be used to capture environmental externalities: those which act to increase greenhouse gas emissions (for example, for coal production) should be reduced and eventually eliminated; those which act to reduce them (for example, for renewable energy development) should be used more proactively.

The interaction of energy pricing policies with the MTS – particularly the WTO-legality of border tax adjustments, and of subsidies applied to reinforce climate change mitigation measures – must be explored and inconsistencies resolved. As in all other areas, a conflict between the climate change regime (and climate change mitigation policies) and the WTO system helps neither trade nor the environment.

Chapter 5

International taxation of bunker fuels

Transport in general is subject to widely varying taxes between different countries. One important component of transport, however, is almost universally exempt from taxation, precisely because of its international nature: the 'bunker fuels' used in international aviation and marine transport. However, the Kyoto Protocol instructs Annex I parties specifically to '... pursue limitation or reduction of emissions of greenhouse gases not controlled by the Montreal Protocol from aviation and marine bunker fuels, working through the International Civil Aviation Organization (ICAO) and the International Maritime Organization (IMO), respectively ...'.[1] The question of the possible application of such taxation is therefore a pertinent one.

International bunker fuels are fuels consumed by air or marine vessels engaged in the international transport of passengers and freight. In total, carbon dioxide emissions from the combustion of international aviation and marine bunker fuels account for approximately 800Mt-CO_2 equivalent, about 4 per cent of global anthropogenic greenhouse gas emissions. Within the transport sector alone, they account for just under 20 per cent of emissions (Figure 5.1).

International shipping is considerably more energy-efficient than is aviation: indeed, it is the most fuel-efficient and least greenhouse-intensive mode of freight transport; air freight has a greenhouse intensity two orders of magnitude greater than that of marine freight (Figure 5.2).

At present, carbon dioxide emissions from the combustion of international aviation and marine bunker fuels are not included within the national emissions inventories of Annex I countries because of difficulties in allocation. Parties to the FCCC have discussed a number of allocation options (see Box 5.1), though most, if not all, are fraught

---

[1] Kyoto Protocol, Article 2.2.

Figure 5.1: Anthropogenic carbon dioxide emissions from the transport sector, 1990

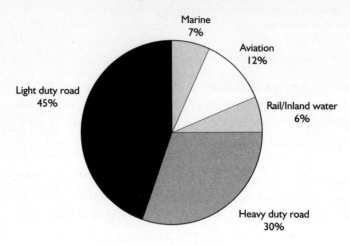

Figure 5.2: Energy intensity of selected transport modes

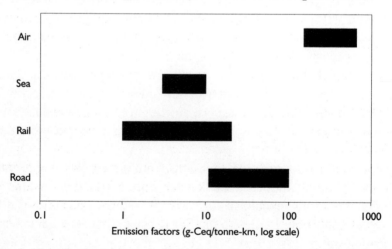

Source: L. Michaelis, *Special Issues in Carbon/Energy Taxation: Marine Bunker Fuel Charges. Project on Policies and Measures for Common Action under the FCCC, Working Paper 11* (Paris: OECD, 1997).

Box 5.1: UNFCCC options for the allocation of emissions from international bunker fuels

Option 1   No allocation.

Option 2   Allocation to parties in proportion to their national emissions.

Option 3   Allocation to parties according to where bunker fuel is sold.

Option 4   Allocation to parties according to nationality of transporting company or to country where the ship or aircraft is registered or to country of operator.

Option 5   Allocation to parties according to the country of departure and destination of aircraft or vessel.

Option 6   Allocation to parties according to country of departure or destination of passenger or cargo.

Option 7   Allocation to parties according to country of origin of passenger or owner of cargo.

Option 8   Allocation to parties of all emissions generated within national borders.

Source: L. Michaelis, *Special Issues in Carbon/Energy Taxation: Marine Bunker Fuel Charges. Project on Policies and Measures for Common Action under the FCCC, Working Paper 11* (Paris: OECD, 1997).

---

with difficulties. More complex still are the means of controlling such emissions once responsibility for them has been allocated. The potential taxation of the sale or consumption of bunker fuels is the topic of this chapter.

5.1 Aviation bunker fuel

Aircraft emit a number of substances that can affect the Earth's climate. Carbon dioxide and water vapour emissions do so directly, while the production of ozone in the troposphere, the alteration of the methane lifetime and modifications to cirrus cloud formation, do so indirectly.[2] In total it is estimated that world civil aviation was responsible for 435Mt-CO_2 equivalent in 1990, approximately 2 per cent of the world's

---

[2] J.H. Ellis, N.R.P. Harris, D.H. Lister and J.E. Penner, *Special Report on Aviation and the Global Atmosphere* (1998).

total anthropogenic carbon dioxide emissions.[3] Aircraft also emit nitrogen oxides (NO_x), carbon monoxide and a range of volatile organic compounds (VOC), depending on a number of factors, such as jet engine performance, the characteristics of the flight and the type of fuel. NO_x emissions, for example, occur during cruise flight and act as a precursor to the formation of ozone in the upper troposphere and lower stratosphere, those altitudes at which the majority of commercial aircraft operate. Emissions from this source are thought to have as significant a radiative impact as that of carbon dioxide.[4] Carbon monoxide and VOC emissions are the product of incomplete combustion and occur during the landing and take-off cycle.

The significance of emissions from the aviation sector lies less in their present contribution than in the forecast growth in air travel between 1990 and 2010.[5] Over the last ten years passenger travel on civil airlines has more than doubled; aviation growth has historically averaged 6 per cent per year between 1980 and 1990. In 1994, the aviation industry comprised some 15,000 aircraft covering 15 million kilometres in scheduled routes servicing nearly 10,000 airports. Over 350 million passengers relied on scheduled airlines for business and tourist travel and over one-third of the value of the world's manufactured products were transported by air, contributing in the process some $1,140 billion to global GNP. Over the next 10–15 years demand for air travel is projected to continue to grow at a similar rate (4.7 per cent per annum) with passenger numbers forecast to reach 573 million by 2002.[6]

---

[3] B. Balashov and A. Smith, 'ICAO Analysis Trends in Fuel Consumption by the World's Airlines', *ICAO Journal*, August 1992.

[4] Commission of the European Communities, *Research and Technology Strategy to Help Overcome the Environmental Problems in Relation to Transport (SAST Project No. 3) Global Pollution Study Report EUR-14713-EN* (Brussels: Commission of the European Communities Directorate General for Science, Research and Development, 1992); and D. Schimel, D. Alves, I. Enting and M. Heimann, 'Radiative Forcing of Climate Change', Houghton et al. (eds), *Climate Change 1995: The Science of Climate Change: Contribution of Working Group I to the Second Assessment Report of the International Panel on Climate Change* (Cambridge University Press, 1996).

[5] G.P. Brasseur, R.A. Cox, D. Hauglustaine, I. Isaksen, J. Levielveld, D.H. Lister, R. Sausen, U. Schumann, A. Wahner and P. Wiesen, 'European Scientific Assessment of the Atmospheric Effects of Aircraft Emissions', *Atmospheric Environment,* 1998.

[6] IATA, *Passenger Forecast 1998–2002* (London: IATA, 1998).

Two fuels dominate commercial airline operations; aviation kero-sene, used by jet and turboprop aircraft and the vast majority of inter-national airlines, and aviation gasoline, used in smaller piston-engined aircraft. Fuel intake does not necessarily take place in the country of departure; long-haul flights typically only take on sufficient fuel to reach their next port of call, whereas on shorter flights aircraft may carry sufficient fuel for several stops and refuel at ports depending upon small differentials in fuel price and other considerations. Fuel costs represent 10–15 per cent of the total operating costs of European carriers, maintaining a strong incentive for improvements in fuel effi-ciency. Technological improvements in airframe aerodynamics, en-gine cycle performance and aircraft weight have all contributed to a steady increase in efficiency of about 2 per cent per annum in recent years. On top of this there are occasional step changes in technology that can achieve 15–20 per cent improvement in one go,[7] such as the 1970s commercialization of the high-bypass turbofan engine and the introduction of wide-body high capacity aircraft. Another such change is under way in the late 1990s, with the commercial deployment of a further generation of engines.

Improvements in energy intensity are forecast to continue over the next two decades at an estimated rate of 2.5–3 per cent per annum. Nevertheless, with air traffic expected to grow at 5–5.5 per cent per annum, total fuel consumption could rise by 65 per cent from 1990–2010.[8] In recent years, one major airline has managed to halve its an-nual fuel consumption per passenger-kilometre but has seen its total fuel consumption double.[9] Nevertheless, at least parts of the aviation industry are currently suggesting voluntary agreements with govern-ment on reducing emissions, mainly to head off the possibility of a new tax. The Association of European Airlines, for example, has agreed a tar-get of a 23 per cent improvement in fuel efficiency by 2010.

---

[7] Energy Technology Support Unit, *Appraisal of UK Energy Research, Development, Demonstration and Dissemination, vol. 7* (HMSO, 1994).

[8] B. Balashov and A. Smith, 'ICAO Analyses Trends in Fuel Consumption by World's Airlines', *ICAO Journal*, August 1992.

[9] H. Somerville, 'Air Quality Issues in the Aviation Industry', *Atmospheric Environment* 31 (1997).

Taxation

The International Civil Aviation Organization was established in 1944 under the Chicago Convention on International Aviation as a specialized agency of the United Nations, with the remit to oversee the development of safe and equitable international air transport services. It currently has 183 contracting states.

The Convention and subsequent ICAO resolutions and recommendations aimed to recognize the unique nature of civil aviation, including the need to accord tax-exempt status to certain aspects of its operation. This rested on the principle of 'reciprocal exemption', which in turn is based, *inter alia*, on long-standing maritime practice. This position has been reinforced by over 2500 bilateral Air Transport Agreements providing explicit exemption from fuel taxes between reciprocating parties. The ICAO does, however, accept the principle that countries can impose an 'environmental charge' on airlines. Airports from Schiphol to Sydney currently impose a noise charge on airlines; Norway introduced a passenger ticket tax in 1995, the so-called 'green tax', on all international flights;[10] and in Switzerland both Zurich and Geneva airports have imposed a landing tax in relation to aircraft NO_x emissions.

EU Environmental Aviation Charge

At present EU aviation fuel benefits from a mandatory exemption from duty and VAT. The Swedish aviation fuel tax introduced in 1991 to encourage airlines to minimize engine emissions, was rescinded when Sweden joined the EU.

In response to growing concern over the impacts of transport, in 1992 the Council decided to review the exclusion of air and sea traffic from indirect taxation and in 1994 concluded that it could not be justi-

---

[10] The unilateral Norwegian introduction of an aviation fuel tax in January 1999, even though this was offset by a reduction in the passenger tax, was met by outrage from foreign airlines, who noted that it broke all the bilateral agreements over fuel taxation. Under threats of non-payment and pressure from other governments, the Norwegian government announced at the end of the month that it would withdraw the new tax and raise the revenue in other ways from air transport.

fied in environmental terms. However, the Council was sensitive to the potential impacts the removal of the exemption would have upon the European aviation industry and made its recommendation conditional upon action taken by competing third parties. The review process culminated in the development of proposals for a European Environmental Aviation Charge, the subject of a comprehensive feasibility study concluding in 1998. The charge is intended to act as an incentive to airlines, and the aviation industry in general, to reduce air pollution – including, though not only, greenhouse gas emissions.

The EU proposal includes five options:

- An emission charge levied on each pollutant emitted by an aircraft while in EU airspace.
- A revenue-neutral emission charge levied on each pollutant emitted by aircraft while European airspace, with revenues recycled to the affected airlines.
- Based upon an emission charge similar to Options 1 and 2 above, but applied only on landing and take-off.
- A complex proposal for three measures in which a fuel charge, as opposed to an emissions charge, plays the central role.
- A movement-based charge paid supplemental to the ticket price.

The charges proposed under each of the five options are equivalent to a $0.10–0.40/l fuel charge, which, based upon a prevailing fuel price of $0.16/l, would lead to a 60–250 per cent increase in aviation fuel prices, resulting in a ticket price rise of approximately $4–5 for a short one-way (500km) trip or $10–15 for a long European flight (2000km).[11] Modelling suggests that a fuel charge of $0.20/l would reduce emissions from aircraft by approximately 30 per cent relative to business as usual, providing an inducement to improve the energy efficiency of the aircraft engine and aircraft design, as well as operational procedures such as speed and altitude adjustments that reduce fuel consumption en route.

---

[11] A.N. Bleijenberg and R.C.N. Wit, *A European Environmental Aviation Charge, Feasibility Study* (Delft: Centre for Energy Conservation and Environmental Technology, 1998).

These price rises are probably large enough to encourage the practice of 'tankering' amongst airlines able to schedule flights to refuel at non-EU ports, or to encourage passengers to choose airports outside the EU in order to avoid the charge. However, provided that the charges are applied in a non-discriminatory manner – i.e. that all carriers, whatever their nationality, would face the same charge – there are unlikely to be any competitiveness impacts, at least in the passenger sector (this may not be true for the freight sector; see below). The impact of the charge on the aviation industry will therefore depend upon the extent to which airlines are able to pass the costs on to their passengers and the means by which the tax revenue is recycled.

The nature of the market and the relative price elasticity of supply and demand on any specific route will determine the extent to which extra costs may be passed on to passengers. However, a survey of airlines undertaken in 1994 indicated that their primary response to a fuel charge would be to reduce non-fuel costs to offset the increase in fuel price.[12] Empirical data collected in the aftermath of the oil shocks of the 1970s suggested that larger fuel price increases were passed on to the customer in the short-term, but absorbed through fuel efficiency improvements in the longer term.[13] The situation is complicated by the oligopolistic nature of the aviation industry, particularly in Europe. Liberalization and the extension of competition may have a larger downwards impact on air transport prices than the imposition of any environmental charge.

5.2 Marine bunker fuel

The issues posed by the allocation and control of greenhouse emissions arising from marine bunker fuels are potentially more complex and intractable than those of the aviation sector. The marine shipping industry comprises some 82,000 vessels of approximately 491 million

---

[12] F.E. Alamdari and D. Brewer, 'Taxation Policy for Aircraft Emissions' *Transport Policy* 1 (3) (1994): 149–59.
[13] T.H. Oum, W.G. Waters and J.S. Yong, 'Concepts of Price Elasticities of Transport Demand and Recent Empirical Estimates: An Interpretative Survey', *Journal of Transport Economics and Policy* 26(2) (1992): 139–54.

tonnes operating around the globe[14] (compared to 15,000 aircraft). The industry is characterized by a complex network of relationships in which a ship owned by a company in one country may be registered in a second, operated by a ship management company in a third, crewed by nationals from a fourth, with carriage paid for by charterers, or in some cases sub-charterers, based in a fifth. Bulk carriers (mainly oil, iron ore, bauxite, coal and grain) account for three-quarters of maritime transport, but only one-quarter of energy use. The greatest proportion of fuel consumption is associated with container ships, Ro-Ro ferries and general cargo ships that operate at greater speeds and energy intensity.

Greenhouse gas emissions from the combustion of marine bunker fuels comprise principally carbon dioxide and water vapour, which contribute 3150g-CO_2 and 1000g-H_2O for every kilogram of fuel consumed. Precursor gases such as nitrogen oxides, sulphur oxides, carbon monoxide and VOCs are also emitted in quantities depending upon the nature of the fuel and the characteristics of combustion. In total, the combustion of marine bunker fuels was estimated to generate in the order of 370Mt-CO_2 equivalent in 1990, rising to 400Mt-CO_2 equivalent in 1994.[15] This equates to just 7 per cent of the total greenhouse emissions generated by the transport sector globally (Figure 5.1).

There are two types of marine fuel – gas oil and fuel oil – which, due to their relatively low cost and ease of handling, are used almost exclusively in the shipping industry. Marine fuels are loaded at any suitable port in the ship's operating schedule, determined in large part by differentials in fuel costs. In total, Annex I countries account for approximately 60 per cent of bunker fuel sales.[16] The United States is the largest supplier (accounting for 20 per cent of world demand), followed by The Netherlands, Japan, Greece, Belgium and Spain.

---

[14] Lloyd's Register of Shipping, *Lloyd's Fleet Statistics 1992* (London: Lloyd's Register of Shipping, 1993).

[15] L. Michaelis, *Special Issues in Carbon/Energy Taxation: Marine Bunker Fuel Charges. Project on Policies and Measures for Common Action under the FCCC, Working Paper 11*, (Paris: OECD, 1997).

[16] Lloyd's Register of Shipping (1993) *Lloyd's Fleet Statistics, 1992* (Lloyd's Register of Shipping, London)

As noted above, international shipping is the most energy efficient and least greenhouse-intensive mode of freight transport. Nevertheless, in recent years energy intensity has been stable, bucking the declining trend evident in most other transport modes. Significant energy efficiency improvements in the 1970s derived not only from technological developments in ship design and propulsion, but also from operational measures such as the increased deployment of information technologies such as the introduction of Global Positioning Systems (GPS) and the use of computer modelling to optimize routing and scheduling.[17] In recent years however, the move away from the practice of 'slow steaming' in the face of increased market pressures and low oil prices, the development of 'just-in-time' manufacturing, which requires more frequent transport of smaller quantities of intermediate goods, and the introduction of ultra-high-speed ships have significantly increased energy consumption on long-haul routes.

Fuel costs are a large proportion of shipping costs and so play an important role in the decisions of ship builders, owners and operators. The fuel share of costs is strongly influenced by vessel type and speed. Higher operating speeds effectively reduce the capital cost of vessels (because the vessel can make more voyages for a fixed capital investment) but at the same time increase the fuel costs (as energy use per kilometre increases with the square of the vessel's speed). Hence the relative importance of fuel costs depends upon the type of vessel and the type of trade in which it is involved. For example, the cost of fuel typically comprises over 30 per cent of total costs for a fully depreciated 15-year-old steam-powered tanker, 20 per cent to 25 per cent of overall capital and operating costs for container ships,[18] but only 10 per cent of overall costs for a new bulk carrier.[19]

---

[17] S. Oftedal, O.M. Martens, H. Ellingsen, and C. Agren, *Air Pollution from Sea Vessels: The Need and Potential for Reductions* (European Federation for Transport and Environment, Brussels, 1996).

[18] R. Wright, *Allocation of Emissions from International Bunker Fuels under the UN Framework Convention on Climate Change* (Oxford: Environmental Resource Management, 1996).

[19] P. Melissen and M. van Mourik, *The Consequences of Environmental Requirements on Fuel Oil Specifications and on Shipping Operational Costs', Marine Systems Design and Operation Paper 13* (London: Marine Management Holdings, 1993).

Projections generally indicate growth in the demand for bunker fuels in the near future, consequent upon growth in marine traffic of between 1 per cent and 2 per cent per annum up to 2010. This would generate emissions of about 600Mt-CO_2 equivalent by 2010, compared with 370Mt-CO_2 equivalent in 1990.

Taxation

The International Maritime Organization plays a role analogous to that of the ICAO in the aviation industry, although its purview is rather broader, overseeing as it does the International Convention for the Prevention of Pollution from Ships (MARPOL Convention). Unlike the ICAO, however, the IMO does not explicitly state in its charter that marine fuels should be exempt from tax or duties, and nor are there a series of bilateral agreements on taxation – but it has been long accepted in practice that ships in transit should be able to take on fuel exempt from local taxes. The EU for example exempts mineral oils used by commercial vessels operating in Community waters from excise duties (though the current Community proposal for an energy products tax, still under discussion, would enable member states to tax domestic and intra-Community journeys by agreement of both member states).

There are few examples of charges imposed upon the marine industry for environmental reasons – largely because of the environmentally benign nature of the industry relative to other modes of transport in terms of energy use and efficiency. Nevertheless, the negotiation of the Kyoto Protocol has raised the issue of taxation of marine bunker fuels; the FCCC's Subsidiary Body for Scientific and Technical Advice (SBSTA) has recently reported to the Annex I Expert Group on the FCCC on the issues associated with the introduction of such a charge.

So far there are relatively few studies of the impact of rising fuel prices on marine transport. Melissen et al. estimated the effects of an increase in the price of marine fuel from \$85/tonne to \$170/tonne, attendant on the introduction of sulphur oxides (SO_x) emission standards; they concluded that a doubling in fuel price would increase bulk transport costs by 10 per cent.[20] Higher fuel costs would of course pro-

---

[20] Ibid.

vide an incentive to improve fuel efficiency: a charge in the order of
$25/tC equivalent might be expected to achieve a reduction in emis-
sions via energy efficiency improvements in engine and ship design, improvements in routing and operating practices, substitution
between vessel types, switching to alternative fuels and an overall
reduction in marine traffic.[21] Such a reduction in fuel use would at
the same time reduce emissions of other pollutants, most notably
SO_x and particulates. Those studies that have quantified the effects
of a marine bunker fuel charge on energy efficiency have suggested
that a doubling of fuel prices relative to 1990 levels could achieve
energy intensity reductions in general cargo shipping in the order of
1 per cent per annum as a result of the accelerated development and
deployment of energy efficient technologies; a further 0.5–1 per
cent might be expected to arise from the introduction of operational
changes such as 'slow steaming', route adjustments and off-shore
loading.[22]

5.3 Taxation of bunker fuels

Clearly, the optimal level for the taxation of bunker fuels is at a global
level. Equally clearly, there are significant political and administrative
barriers to this application. Given the urgency of the climate change
issues, therefore, it is worth exploring what costs and benefits would
arise from sub-global – for example, EU – taxation.

Feasibility

The international aviation and shipping industries both operate between various tax jurisdictions, and a considerable proportion of their
operations occurs outside the scope of any national authority. In the

---

[21] L. Michaelis, *Special Issues in Carbon/Energy Taxation: Marine Bunker Fuel Charges. Project on Policies and Measures for Common Action under the FCCC, Working Paper 11* (Paris: OECD, 1997).
[22] S. Oftedal, O.M. Martens, H. Ellingsen and C. Agren, *Air Pollution from Sea Vessels: The Need and Potential for Reductions* (Brussels: European Federation for Transport and Environment, 1996).

absence of coordinated international action on taxation, therefore, the question of 'tankering' to avoid payment of the tax is relevant.

Fuel intake by airlines does not necessarily take place in the country of departure. Since carrying excess fuel increases the weight of the aircraft, airlines on long-haul flights usually take on only that amount of fuel necessary to reach their destination. On such routes there is little opportunity to re-route flights. On short-haul flights, however, aircraft may and do carry sufficient fuel for several stops, uplifted from ports depending upon fuel prices and other considerations. Thus it may be feasible in certain circumstances and on certain routes to avoid, say, EU charges on aviation fuel by uplifting that fuel from hub airports outside the Community's jurisdiction. 'Tankering', where an aircraft takes on more fuel than is needed for a flight to avoid taking on a more expensive or lower quality fuel at the next port of call, already occurs to some extent; indeed, airlines have developed software to plan their refuelling operations on the basis of even very small differentials in fuel price and quality. However, the very nature of air travel, its frequency and time dependence, make significant diversions on the basis of fuel charges unrealistic except on certain short-haul routes.

This is not the case in the international shipping industry, however, where the risk of avoidance of a sub-global tax is very real. As discussed above, fuel costs contribute a significant proportion of operating costs in the international shipping industry and ships already choose their bunker fuel suppliers on the basis of small differentials in price. Marine fuels are not necessarily loaded at the outset of the voyage, but they may be taken on at any convenient time in the vessel's operating schedule. Offshore bunker supply is already normal practice in order to avoid paying port fees or being constrained by loading limits in specific ports. Thus the imposition of even a modest marine bunker fuel charge of $5/tonne has the potential to encourage owners and operators to bunker at ports outside the coverage of the charge. The cost of transporting fuel from a port in Africa or the Middle East to northern Europe, for example, or from Latin America to North America is of the order of $10–15/tonne. The imposition of a charge greater than this level would provide an incentive for suppliers to transport untaxed fuel to supply points immediately outside the national waters of these countries. Owing to the distance between ports and the transitory nature of the industry, ship owners and operators have considerable flexibility in choosing bunkering locations. Thus, in the market for marine fuels, unlike aviation fuels, only a global charge would be fully effective.

Competitiveness

What impact would the imposition of bunker fuel taxes have on the competitiveness of the industries? This is an important question for sectors where fuel costs account for 15–30 per cent of overall costs, as they do in international aviation and marine transport, and where taxes may be applied sub-globally.

The European Federation of Transport and Environment's study on the potential competitiveness impacts of the proposed EU aviation charge (see section 5.1) on EU carriers[23] identified three broad categories in which some distortion might be evident: between EU and non-EU carriers; between EU and non-EU airports; and between the EU and non-EU tourist industries. Of the five options that the study investigated, the adoption of a fuel charge appeared to lead to the most significant distortions in the industry, including airlines, airports and the tourist industry in general. The study concluded, however, that the potential competitiveness impact on charters and low-cost carriers would be negligible, and while the impact upon EU scheduled carriers could be marginally higher, it was unlikely to be significant in the context of market liberalization and consolidation within the industry. A fuel charge could potentially result in a more significant distortion for airports and the tourism industry as evasion led to shifts in the origin and destination of flights to hubs outside Community jurisdiction. A particularly onerous charge might be expected to encourage 'tankering' practices on certain routes where feasible – likely to be more evident for freight than for passenger transport.

---

[23] A.N. Bleijenberg and R.C.N Wit, *Potential Economic Distortions of a European Environmental Aviation Charge* (Delft: Centre for Energy Conservation and Environmental Technology, 1997).

The competitiveness impact of a sub-global marine bunker fuel charge on the international shipping industry is likely to be more serious, as illustrated by the experiences of the US West Coast bunker fuel market. In 1991, an 8.5 per cent sales tax was imposed upon bunker fuel. Before the introduction of the tax the Los Angeles/Long Beach bunker market was amongst the largest and most profitable bunker-only ports in the world; approximately 4.5 million barrels of bunker fuel were sold every month. Following the introduction of the tax, trade volumes dropped significantly, reaching a low of 1 million barrels per month in July 1992, shortly before the tax was rescinded; the market has since recovered, though only to approximately 1.5 million barrels per month. The tax remains the subject of ongoing legislation in California, where the state legislature is considering its re-introduction. The Pacific Merchant Shipping Association claims that by re-introducing such a tax, bunker sales in the state would decline by a further 50 per cent, with the principal beneficiary being the Panama bunker market.

As explored in Chapter 4, there are, of course, means of minimizing the competitiveness pressures of such a charge, for example through revenue recycling. However, the countries and carriers whose trade would be affected by charges are not necessarily those which would collect the revenues. If the tax were placed on bunker fuel sales within Annex I countries, for example, over 90 per cent of the revenue would be collected by the United States, The Netherlands and Japan, while almost 60 per cent of global fuel sales would be exempt from the charge. In contrast, if the tax were collected from Annex I ship owners on the basis of origin of registration, approximately 75 per cent of the revenue would accrue to Greece, Norway and Japan, while more than 79 per cent of the world's fleet would be exempt.

Substitution

The final issue to be considered is the impact of environmental taxes or charges on switching between transport modes. As Figure 5.2 indicated, rail and marine transport are significantly the most energy-efficient modes, while air transport is significantly the least efficient. In comparison with cargo transported by road for example, shipping is approximately five times more energy-efficient. Although the issue is complicated by widely varying levels of taxation on other transport modes (road and rail), any measure which raises the cost of marine transport while not at the same time raising the costs of other modes is likely to be environmentally negative. In markets such as Europe and North America, where marine and road transport compete with one another, switching freight from land to sea could have potentially significant implications for energy use in the transport sector. The imposition of a tax on marine bunker fuels in such markets therefore, would simply encourage a switch to more, rather than less, energy-intensive transport modes. Substitution away from aviation, however, is almost certain to reduce energy use. The scope for this varies substantially by region, of course, and is limited to high-density, short-haul routes which could or do have coach or rail links. Estimates suggest that up to 10 per cent of travellers in Europe could be transferred from aircraft to high-speed trains.[24]

Conclusion

The taxation of international bunker fuels poses difficult questions of feasibility connected with the international scope and operations of the aviation and marine transport industries. The discussions set out in this chapter tend to lead towards three conclusions:

- The removal of the tax exemption for international bunker fuels will be most effective if it is applied at a global level; this is probably unlikely in the short term.
- Given this, and given the high levels of energy efficiency of marine transport and the high propensity of ship operators to move between different suppliers, there is very little advantage to be gained in seeking to apply sub-global taxation to marine bunker fuels.
- Given the much lower levels of fuel efficiency in the aviation industry, the lower likelihood of tankering and the anticipated rapid

---

[24] Special Report of Working Groups I and III of the IPCC, 'Aviation and the Global Atmosphere' (April 1999), section 6.4.

growth in air transport, there are advantages to be gained from sub-global taxation (for example at EU level) of aviation bunker fuels in some form.

Chapter 6

Flexibility mechanisms and trade

The 'flexibility mechanisms' of the Kyoto Protocol – the emissions trading system (Article 17), joint implementation (JI) (Article 6), and the clean development mechanism (CDM) (Article 12) – form together some of the most interesting aspects of the agreement. They represent, for the first time in an international environmental treaty, the wholesale utilization of market-based mechanisms for environmental ends. If implemented fully, they should lead to the creation of an entirely new global market, in the right to emit (and the commitment to control) greenhouse gases.

Under the Protocol, Annex I countries (broadly speaking, the industrialized world) are required to reduce greenhouse emissions by approximately 800MtC by the period 2008–2012. Assuming that 50 per cent of these emission reductions are achieved through domestic action, and estimating a carbon abatement cost of $50/tC, this represents a potential market of $20 billion per year, equivalent to about 0.5 per cent of the current value of developed country exports – a significant sum for an entirely artificial market.[1]

Since the Protocol aims to utilize trading mechanisms, an obvious question to ask is to what extent these are likely to be compatible with the multilateral trading system. Very little attention has been paid to this question to date – a situation which can be expected to change as implementation dates for the emissions trading and CDM draw closer (certified emissions reductions under the CDM can start to accumulate from the year 2000). The aim of this chapter is to explore the issues at stake. Section 6.1 examines the inter-relationship between the MTS and emissions trading. Section 6.2 looks briefly at the even more speculative

---

[1] Estimates of the scale of transfers and the costs of abatement vary widely, and the figures used here are indicative only – for a fuller discussion, see M. Grubb et al., *The Kyoto Protocol: A Guide and Assessment*, Chapter 5.

interaction between the CDM and possible future WTO agreements on international investment.

6.1 Emissions trading and the multilateral trading system[2]

The system described in outline in Article 17 of the Kyoto Protocol envisages parties to the treaty – i.e., governments – participating in the trading. It is generally assumed, however, that if an international emissions trading system is to operate effectively, it must be extended to the private sector – i.e. governments allocate permits to companies, which may then be traded with other companies, both domestic and foreign, probably through exchanges. Articles 6, on JI, and 12, on the CDM, both explicitly recognize that private entities may participate. The potential inter-relationship with the WTO can then be considered under four headings:

1. Will the emissions units which are to be traded be recognizable items under the WTO?
2. Will the trading system itself fall under WTO disciplines?
3. Does the initial allocation system for emissions permits raise WTO-related questions?
4. Can emissions reduction units traded under Articles 6 and 17, and certified emissions reductions generated from the CDM (Article 12) be considered to be 'like products'?

Are emissions units recognizable items under the WTO?
Will the emissions units which are to be traded be recognisable items under the WTO? They may not be: not every aspect of international commerce is covered by the multilateral trading system, including trade in electricity, in oil (excluded from the GATT because of its international security implications) and in money – a possible parallel to

---

[2] Relatively little has yet been written on the questions covered in this section. For further discussion, however, see Richard B. Stewart, Jonathan B. Wiener and Philippe Sands, *Legal Issues Presented by a Pilot International Greenhouse Gas Trading System* (Geneva: UNCTAD, 1996); and Zhong Xiang Zhang, 'Greenhouse Gas Emission Trading and the World Trading System', *Journal of World Trade* 32:5, October 1998.

emissions units, which have no value in themselves, being representations of the holder's right to do something (for money, to purchase goods and services; for emissions units, to emit greenhouse gases). WTO members would need to take a positive decision to bring emissions trading in under the multilateral trading system, an eventuality which is possible (see below) but not automatic.[3]

If emissions units are considered to be 'goods' under the WTO system, the standard WTO disciplines of non-discrimination and openness would apply. This should not lead to any difficulties as long as the emissions trading system is open to unlimited participation from all countries (or, at least, all WTO members). If the membership of the system is restricted, however – which of course it is, to Annex I parties (explicitly in Articles 6 and 17) – this would potentially lead to a conflict, in which case a WTO dispute panel could find itself in the position of considering whether or not the restriction of the system was necessary to the achievement of the environmental objective, or whether less discriminatory options were available.

It should be emphasized at this point, however, that a simple *potential* for conflict is not necessarily a worry. It only becomes actual if a WTO member decides to start the dispute settlement process; it is at that point that a WTO dispute panel would have to decide on issues such as the treatment of emissions units under the WTO agreements. The important question is therefore whether it is likely that any WTO member would initiate such a dispute; in this context, it might presumably be a non-Annex I party wishing to gain access to the emissions trading system without itself being listed in Annex I of the Protocol. This is perhaps not totally inconceivable, but it does seem highly unlikely; non-Annex I enterprises could, after all quite legitimately buy and sell emissions units as long as they are generated and verified in Annex I countries.

---

[3] It is worth noting in passing that if emissions units were to be considered to be equivalent to capital assets, they would probably be subject to financial regulations administered by national Securities Exchange Commissions or similar bodies.

Will the trading system itself fall under WTO disciplines?

The second question is whether the trading system itself – the infrastructure of brokers and exchanges – might be considered to be 'services' under the General Agreement on Trade in Services (GATS). One of the Uruguay Round agreements, the GATS aims to provide legally enforceable rights to trade in all services, and has a built-in commitment to continuous liberalization through periodic negotiations. Its core principles of non-discrimination between national and foreign service providers, and between different members of the agreement, are essentially the same as those of the GATT. It also has an exceptions clause (Article XIV), which includes a GATT-type exception for measures 'necessary to protect human, animal or plant life or health'[4] though *not* an exception for measures 'relating to the conservation of exhaustible natural resources'.[5]

Specific services are themselves defined in annexes to the GATS, and the Annex on Financial Services includes the following:

> For the purposes of this Annex:
> (a)   ... Financial services include the following activities ...
> (x)   Trading for own account or for account of customers, whether on an exchange, in an over-the-counter-market or otherwise, the following:
>   ...
>   (C) derivative products including, but not limited to, futures and options;
>   ...
>   (E) transferable securities;
>   (F) other negotiable instruments and financial assets;
> (xi) Participation in issues of all kinds of securities, including underwriting and placement as agent (whether publicly or privately) and provision of services related to such issues.[6]

It seems likely that emissions units could be considered to fall under one or more of these definitions, being in practice transferable securi-

---

[4] GATS Article XIV (b).

[5] A potentially important omission, as it was on this paragraph (Article XX(g)) in the GATT which the Appellate Body rested its ruling in the shrimp-turtle case.

[6] GATS Annex on Financial Services, 5(a)(x) and (xi).

ties with all the characteristics of derivative instruments. As above, however, all this means is that traders and exchanges based in any country, whether or not they are Annex I members, should be allowed to enter the market – and there is no good environmental reason why they should not. Indeed, the application of WTO disciplines to this new activity may well be helpful in providing regulatory oversight. In any case, the GATS has evolved in practice in a very gradual manner, with governments opting in to those sectors they consider suitable (there is no absolute definition of a 'service'). It seems likely that the inclusion of emissions trading in the GATS would only be the result of a positive decision to do so – i.e. it would not happen automatically.

Does the initial allocation system for emissions permits raise WTO-related questions?

The initial allocation of permits under the emissions trading system could fall under the provisions of the multilateral trading system – in this case, under the Agreement on Subsidies and Countervailing Measures. As noted in Section 4.5, the SCM Agreement's definition of a 'subsidy' is where: '(a)(1) there is a financial contribution by a government or any public body within the territory of a Member … i.e. where …. (iii) government provides goods or services other than general infrastructure, or purchases goods …. and (b) a benefit is thereby conferred'.[7]

Whether this applies to greenhouse gas emission permits is not clear. Is a permit a 'financial contribution'? If permits are grandfathered (i.e. given away to firms by the government), a strong case can be made that this in practice *does* represent the creation of financial assets, and the SCM Agreement is therefore applicable. If they are auctioned (i.e. firms purchase them from the government), then this could hardly be regarded as a 'financial contribution'. Auctioning is the economically optimal form of allocation, so it is not surprising that this should create no problems for a trade liberalization agreement, which also seeks economic optimality. Grandfathering, which can be viewed as a new way

---

[7] Agreement on Subsidies and Countervailing Measures, Article 1, para 1.1.

to grant subsidies, in a sense *should* cause problems – and, since for clear political reasons this is the most likely way to allocate permits, this is the most likely reason to bring about an interaction with the WTO.

If grandfathering is subject to the SCM Agreement, then the allocation process would become subject to GATT-type principles of non-discrimination: it must meet the Agreement's requirements for non-specificity, i.e. it must not be 'specific to an enterprise or industry or group of enterprises or industries ... within the jurisdiction of the granting authority'.[8] This would seem to imply that any enterprise operating within a government's jurisdiction should have the same rights of access to permits as any other, regardless of the nationality of its ownership. This need not create any problem for the emissions trading system, since each party must be able to control emissions emanating from any enterprise operating within its territory. It would rule out, however, any favourable treatment of domestic industry over foreign industry operating in the same jurisdiction in permit allocation. It could also rule out any arbitrary treatment of different sectors of industry in allocating permits. There are implications for new entrants to an industry – which would have to be guaranteed access to the permit system in some way – and there may also be implications for the transfer of permits between, for example, different national components of a transnational corporation.

Can emissions reductions units and certified emissions reductions be considered to be 'like products'?

There are a number of inconsistencies between emissions units traded under Article 17 of the Protocol and certified emission reductions (CERs) generated under the CDM – partly due to the slightly haphazard way in which the text of the Protocol was finally settled. In particular, early crediting (from 2000) is allowed for the CDM, but not for emissions trading. Most of the details of both schemes remain to be worked out, and are the subject of ongoing international negotiations.

---

[8] Ibid., Article 2, para 2.1.

One important issue is whether emissions reduction units and CERs are equivalent to each other, or fungible. It seems likely that they will be; Article 3 lists all the three sources of emissions units,[9] and Article 12 states that 'parties included in Annex I may use the CERs accruing from such project activities to contribute to compliance with part of their ... commitments under Article 3 ... .'[10] There is, however, a possibility of discounting the CERs depending on risk factors. If emissions trading and the CDM in general are to be considered subject to WTO disciplines, then it is quite likely that, in the event of a dispute, a WTO panel would consider them to be 'like products' under Article I of the GATT. If so, any differential treatment of emissions units and CERs would be incompatible with the WTO, reinforcing the case for fungibility.[11]

Conclusion

The various agreements comprising the multilateral trading system, and the Kyoto Protocol (when in force) are legal documents, but they are also political agreements. It is possible to speculate on the relationship between them, but in the final analysis these questions will probably be settled by negotiation between the parties to both sets of treaties. The fact that the climate change negotiations have tended to include representatives of trade as well as of environment departments from most governments, potentially makes this relationship (often rather strained in the case of other environmental treaties) easier.

The question that should be asked is therefore whether the aims of trade liberalization and of environmental protection are best served by keeping the WTO and the Protocol separate, or by bringing them together. Unless it can be shown that WTO disciplines may interfere with the aims of the Protocol – which may possibly be the case with permit allocation systems, but appears not to be the case elsewhere – then the involvement of the highly-evolved and effective WTO system in the

---

[9] Kyoto Protocol, Article 3.10–3.12.

[10] Kyoto Protocol, Article 12(3)(b).

[11] For other reasons why it is desirable that emissions reduction units and CERs should be compatible, see Grubb et al., *The Kyoto Protocol*, Chapter 6.

new global emissions market to be created under the Kyoto Protocol could well be positive.

6.2 The flexibility mechanisms and international investment

The clean development mechanism (CDM) potentially creates an important proxy market for carbon abatement in developing countries. Considering the illustrative figures used in the introduction to this chapter, if an 'emissions market' of $20 billion per year develops, it is conceivable that 25 per cent of this may be generated by CDM credits – a sum of $5 billion a year. While small in proportion to total world trade, this still represents the equivalent of about 0.4 per cent of the current value of developing country exports and 7.5 per cent of the value of overseas development assistance. This is a significant sum.

How would the CDM be treated under the multilateral trading system?[12] Section 6.1 has already considered the trade in emissions credits generated by CDM investments. But what about the investments themselves? The Uruguay Round included a rudimentary investment agreement, the WTO Agreement on Trade-Related Investment Measures (TRIMS Agreement). It sought to extend the GATT principles of national treatment and the elimination of quantitative restrictions to investment measures related to trade in goods. Trade-related investment measures not in conformity with these principles were to be notified to the WTO Council and eliminated within two years of the entry into force of the Agreement (or five years for developing countries and seven years for least developed countries).

The TRIMS Agreement is quite limited in application. The Multilateral Agreement on Investment (MAI), which the OECD attempted to negotiate between 1995 and 1998, was much wider. It aimed to apply national treatment and most favoured nation principles to investments and investors, provide a high standard of protection to foreign investors and investments when operating overseas and constrain host governments' ability to extend requirements (for instance for technology

---

[12] The arguments in this section also largely apply to emissions reduction units generated under JI (Article 6 of the Protocol).

transfer or local employment) to foreign investors even where this was not discriminatory as between domestic and foreign investors. Countries were to be permitted to specify sectors of their economies to which MAI disciplines would not apply (though the hope was that these would prove temporary derogations only). The MAI covered virtually every type of investment, including intangible assets, state authorizations or licences, claims to money and all kinds of contractual rights, and was backed by a dispute settlement procedure which allowed investors to challenge states directly.

The MAI negotiations eventually collapsed in late 1998. Growing concern had been expressed at the potential impact of its provisions on governments' ability to maintain high standards of environmental and labour protection and to promote local and regional development, at the possible interaction between the MAI and MEAs and at the lack of any additional responsibilities for investors (such as a requirement to implement high environmental standards) to balance their additional rights (the OECD's guidelines for transnational enterprises were to be appended to the agreement, but were only to be voluntary in application). In the face of a vociferous NGO campaign, a lack of strong support from most businesses, the awareness that developing countries, to whom MAI disciplines would inevitably eventually apply yet who were not present in the negotiations, and unease amongst governments at the implications, the talks were first frozen and then officially abandoned. Much interest was expressed, however, in the injection into the Millennium Round of further talks on a new WTO investment agreement.

In what ways would the MAI, if adopted and implemented, have interacted with the CDM?[13] CDM project activity clearly falls under the MAI's definition of investment, and it would therefore apply in the territory of any developing country that chose to accede to the agreement. The MAI's definition of an investor would extend its rights to

---

[13] This section largely follows Jacob Werksman and Claudia Santoro, 'Investing in Sustainable Development: The Potential Interaction between the Kyoto Protocol and the Multilateral Agreement on Investment', in W. Bradnee Chambers (ed.), *Global Climate Governance: Inter-linkages between the Kyoto Protocol and Other Multilateral Regimes* (Tokyo: United Nations University, 1998).

enterprises (though not states) involved in CDM transactions. Potential sources of conflict can be identified as follows:

Non-discrimination

The MAI's core principles of non-discrimination could become relevant in a number of instances:

- If non-Annex I party investors were to be excluded from CDM activities; Article 12 of the Kyoto Protocol does not specifically prohibit this, but it does imply that the investment should come from Annex I parties.
- Similarly, if non-party investors were to be excluded, which, again, is not explicit, but can be inferred as a logical requirement.
- If attempts were made as part of a non-compliance mechanism to bar investors from non-complying parties (see Chapter 7).
- If the host country attempted to place restrictions on foreign investments in CDM projects, reserving them for domestic investors – perhaps to allow time for domestic industry to develop enough to compete with foreign competitors.

In all these cases, the investor discriminated against would have a clear case under MAI provisions.

Performance requirements

It is easy to imagine particular performance requirements, such as for technology transfer, or the employment of local workers, being placed on CDM activities by host countries – Article 12 of the Protocol, after all, states that the purpose of the CDM is to assist developing country parties in achieving sustainable development. Even if imposed equally on all investors, domestic and foreign, any such requirements could violate the MAI. The agreement did include a 'saving clause', modelled on Article XX of the GATT, which would allow such measures if it could be shown that they were 'necessary for the conservation of living or non-living exhaustible natural resources', but the objectives of economic and technological development seem unlikely to fall into this category.

Expropriation and compensation

The MAI's definition of 'expropriation' is a wide one, covering regulatory takings, or state measures such as taxation and licensing, as well as straightforward confiscation – it aimed to prohibit the taking of any state action or measure that had the equivalent effect of direct or indirect nationalization or 'creeping' expropriation. If host countries attempted to impose, as part of CDM activities, taxes or regulations which could qualify as expropriation in this way, there is a potential clash with the MAI.

There is also the issue of the destination of the certified emission reductions (CERs) generated by the CDM investment. It has been suggested that host countries should be entitled to a portion of the CERs as a 'resource rent' for providing the regulatory framework necessary for the investment to take place. Again, this could be regarded as expropriation under the MAI.

Conclusions

These considerations are entirely hypothetical: the MAI has been abandoned and it seems highly unlikely that the OECD will take it up again. But it is conceivable that an international agreement on investment will be negotiated in some forum – quite possibly the WTO – at some point in the future. The potential for clashes between the MAI and the CDM (and, more widely, other MEAs) should provide some valuable lessons for the design of any such future agreement.

Chapter 7

Trade measures and the Kyoto Protocol

The final set of topics to be examined is the potential implications for the multilateral trading system of any restrictions on trade which may potentially be required by the Kyoto Protocol. This chapter is the most speculative in this book; no such requirements exist at present, but it is at least possible that some may develop in the future.

The experience of the ozone regime – the 1987 Montreal Protocol on Substances that Deplete the Ozone Layer, and its subsequent adjustments and amendments – shows that two kinds of trade measures were developed in the process of implementing its requirements:

1. Trade bans with non-parties, required by the treaty as an enforcement mechanism.
2. Trade restrictions between parties, adopted in order to implement the control schedules.

Sections 7.2 and 7.3 of this chapter describe these provisions and consider their application to the Kyoto Protocol. Before that, however, we begin with an outline of the existing non-compliance mechanisms in the Convention and Protocol.

7.1 Non-compliance provisions in the climate change regime

It is almost an exaggeration to say that the non-compliance provisions of the climate change regime are in their infancy – they are not really yet developed that far.

Article 13 of the UNFCCC calls for the consideration of a 'multilateral consultative process ... for the resolution of questions regarding the implementation of the Convention'. The climate change issue, and the concept of enforcement of any obligations relating to emissions reductions, was highly sensitive at the time of negotiation of the Convention (and still is), and many parties, including developing countries and the US, were determined to avoid what they perceived to be the relatively strict Montreal Protocol model of non-compliance regime. The Ad Hoc Group on Article 13 (AG13) was established under the Berlin Mandate in 1995 (see Chapter 1) to develop the process. In the course of fulfilling its mandate, it moved increasingly in the direction of an advisory, rather than a supervisory, regime, aiming to provide a 'help desk'[1] to parties facing difficulty in fulfilling their obligations. AG13 completed its work in mid-1998, and the conference of the parties in Buenos Aires was able to agree on most of the suggested text, with the exception of the composition of the implementation committee to be established to oversee the process. This proved controversial (mainly because of the precedent it would set for other committees established under the Protocol) and a decision was delayed until 1999.

In addition to Article 13, Article 14 makes provision for dispute settlement, providing for an arbitration procedure (possibly through the International Court of Justice) and a conciliation commission, to be created where necessary.

The Protocol itself contains three relevant articles: 16, which instructs the parties to consider the application of the Convention's multilateral consultative process to the Protocol; 18, which requires the first meeting of the parties (after the entry into force of the Protocol) 'to approve appropriate and effective procedures and mechanisms to determine and to address cases of non-compliance with the provisions of the Protocol'; and 19, which adopts the dispute settlement procedures of the Convention. The articles which define the flexibility mechanisms (emissions trading, the clean development mechanism and joint implementation) contain no reference themselves to compliance and enforcement (apart from the reference in Article 6 to parties in non-compliance not being able to use emission reduction units generated through joint implementation to meet their commitments), but it is widely recognized that there must be some form of policing for the

---

[1] For this phrase, and for an incisive analysis of the evolution to date of the climate change non-compliance regime, I am indebted to Patrick Szell (UK DETR), personal communication.

trading to take place; it is essential that the systems are not undermined by trades in permits which do not accurately represent valid emissions reductions.

As with the debates within AG13, the EU has been the strongest proponent of a tough non-compliance mechanism, and one capable of dealing comprehensively (i.e. though a single process, with a single implementation committee) with all the different questions of non-compliance that may arise, including those connected with emissions trading. It is not at all clear, however, what the penalties for non-compliance could potentially be – and the requirement, in Article 18, for any 'procedures and mechanisms ... entailing binding consequences' to be adopted as an amendment to the Protocol, places another significant barrier in their way. In contrast, the US and some other countries have argued for individual mechanisms to be developed under the different articles – starting with Article 17 (emissions trading) and moving on to the rest (though how long it would take to get round to 'the rest' is an interesting question). One significant problem for either of these approaches, however, is the still-undeveloped nature of all the articles in question; it is clearly difficult to devise a non-compliance mechanism when one does not know precisely what countries will have to do to comply.

Resolution of the issue will be a slow process, though there are signs that countries' positions are moving closer together, with the EU, for example, accepting that within a single process there could be a useful role for different channels, one of an administrative and technical nature, leading to the provision of advice and assistance, and another of a quasi-judicial nature, leading ultimately to penalties. The Buenos Aires conference resolved that discussions would be concluded by the sixth conference of the parties in 2000. In one sense, there is no need to hurry. Since the first commitment period under the Protocol is 2008–2012, and full data would not then be available until 2013 at the earliest, there would be no scope for a non-compliance procedure to take effect until, probably, 2014. On the other hand, however, the flexibility mechanisms are designed to begin operation much earlier than this, and the Protocol contains requirements for data reporting which start immediately it comes into force, so these all add to the pressure for early decision.

Given this background, what scope is there for the use of Montreal Protocol-type trade measures?

7.2 The use of trade measures as an enforcement mechanism

Trade measures in the Montreal Protocol

The Montreal Protocol uses trade measures as one policy instrument among several in achieving its aim of protecting the ozone layer. Parties to the treaty are required to ban trade with non-parties in ozone-depleting substances (ODS), such as CFCs, in products containing them, such as refrigerators, and, potentially, in products made with but not containing CFCs, such as electronic components (though this provision has not yet been implemented primarily because of problems of detection, and also because of the small volumes of CFCs involved). These trade measures have been gradually extended to all the categories of ozone-depleting substances covered by the Montreal Protocol, the final substance, methyl bromide, being added at the meeting of the parties in September 1997.

The trade measures were included in the treaty as an enforcement mechanism. They had two aims. One was to maximize participation in the Protocol, by shutting off non-signatories from supplies of CFCs and providing a significant incentive to join. If completely effective, this would in practice render the trade provisions redundant, as there would be no non-parties against which to apply them.

The other goal, should participation not prove total, was to prevent industries from migrating to non-signatory countries to escape the phase-out schedules. In the absence of trade restrictions, not only could this fatally undermine the control measures, but it would help non-signatory countries to gain a competitive advantage over signatories, as the progressive phase-outs raised industrial production costs. If trade was forbidden, however, non-signatories would not only be unable to export CFCs, but would also be unable to enjoy fully the potential gains from cheaper production as exports of products containing, and eventually made with, CFCs, would also be restricted.

All the evidence suggests that the trade provisions achieved their objectives. All CFC-producing countries, and all but a handful of consuming nations, have adhered to the treaty. Although it is difficult to determine states' precise motivations for joining – there are a variety of reasons, including the availability of financial support for developing countries – that trade restrictions do appear to have provided a powerful incentive, and a number of countries have cited them as the major justification.[2]

The question of whether the trade measures can be used against a party which is in non-compliance with the treaty is now arising. So far there has only been one instance of persistent non-compliance – the Russian Federation, which failed to achieve phase-out of CFC production and consumption by the Protocol deadline of 1 January 1996, and has still not done so. The current non-compliance procedure of the Protocol tries to avoid confrontation, and the emphasis has been on working with the Russian government to improve implementation (while withholding financial support until full data was provided) – with some results. Some dissatisfaction, however, has been expressed at the slow pace of this process, with at least some countries pressing for the use or threat of trade measures to be incorporated at an earlier stage in the process.

In any case, the availability of trade measures as a sanction of last resort is an important underpinning of the non-compliance procedure. Total or partial bans on trade have been employed as an enforcement mechanism, with success, in the Convention on International Trade in Endangered Species (CITES).[3] In a number of cases where countries have been identified as being in persistent non-compliance, the Standing Committee of the CITES conference has recommended all parties to apply Article XIV(1) of the Convention, which allows parties to take stricter domestic measures than those provided by the treaty, including complete prohibitions of trade, collectively (albeit temporarily) against the offending countries. This has included the United Arab Emirates in 1985–90, Thailand in 1991–2 and Italy in 1992–3. The procedure has also been used against states not party to the Convention, after persis-

---

[2] For a full description of the trade measures and their efficacy, see Duncan Brack, *International Trade and the Montreal Protocol* (London: RIIA/Earthscan, 1996).

[3] See Peter H. Sand, 'Whither CITES? The Evolution of a Treaty Regime in the Borderland of Trade and Environment', *European Journal of International Law* 8 (1997), pp. 29–58.

tent refusal to provide 'comparable documents' to CITES licenses; in the case of El Salvador (1986–7) and Equatorial Guinea (1988–92), the ban was lifted after the countries targeted became parties.

In the Montreal Protocol and CITES, therefore, the ability to restrict trade has proved of value both in persuading non-parties to adhere to the regime and as a sanction against non-complying parties.

Application to the Kyoto Protocol

In principle, similar provisions may form an important component of future MEAs with similar aims, i.e. of placing limits on the production and consumption of polluting substances or behaviour. This applies to MEAs which, like the Montreal Protocol, may use trade measures as an enforcement and compliance mechanism alongside other policy instruments – phase-out schedules, financial and technology transfer, etc. – in achieving their aims. The Kyoto Protocol is an example, as is the forthcoming UNEP convention on the control of persistent organic pollutants.

Three sets of issues need to be examined when considering the value of such trade measures in any given MEA:

1. Feasibility.
2. Fairness.
3. Interrelationship with the multilateral trading system.

Feasibility

Montreal Protocol-type trade measures, i.e. bans on trade, will be easiest to implement if the products being controlled are:

(a) limited in type and application;
(b) limited in origin;
(c) easily detectable; and
(d) easily substitutable.

In the case of the ozone regime, the main (Annex A) CFCs fitted this bill quite well. Only a limited number of producers in a small number of countries manufactured them; although this range widens when products containing CFCs are considered, it still forms a not very substantial proportion of world trade, or of any single country's exports and imports. Note that the limits are much looser when products made with but not containing CFCs are added – which is one of the reasons why the parties decided not to implement this section of the Protocol (though the volume of CFCs which would have been affected was also quite limited). CFCs can be hidden, and are difficult to detect, requiring, for example, chemical analysis to prove their presence if their containers are mislabelled. Indeed, illegal trade is a growing problem for the implementation of the Protocol, but the steps taken by the US (and, recently, EU) authorities to tackle the problem show that it can be countered quite effectively. Finally, CFCs have turned out to be relatively easy to substitute – one of the main reasons why the Protocol has proved to be such a success – so any argument against trade measures resting on the dependence of any country on trade in CFCs is not strong. For all these reasons, trade measures in the Protocol are both technically and politically feasible.

Rather greater problems are encountered in applying these tests to the case of climate change. Greenhouse gases, of course, are not precisely analogous to ODS, since most of them – carbon dioxide, some sources of methane, nitrous oxide – are essentially byproducts, whereas others – HFCs,[4] some PFCs – are themselves products which are traded. For this latter group, Montreal Protocol-type trade restrictions could be applied, and the issues and problems are very similar.

For the former, and much more important, category, trade restrictions would have to be applied against either the commodities which release greenhouse gases when used – i.e. fossil fuels – and/or goods made with processes which release greenhouse gases, which in practice means the vast majority of manufactured goods. These largely fail all the four tests set out above: they are not limited in type or origin,

---

[4] The use of HFCs is also of interest to the parties to the Montreal Protocol, since they are non-ozone depleting substitutes for CFCs and other ozone-depleting substances in a range of refrigeration and other uses. There is a clear need for each MEA to avoid conflict with each other, and during 1998 the conference or meeting of the parties of each agreement adopted decisions stressing the need for close coordination.

they are not easily detectable, and they are not easily substitutable. However, this case is not quite the same as the Montreal Protocol. Since ultimate phase-out of greenhouse gases is not the aim, it may be that total trade bans might not so appropriate; duties or taxes, for example, could be applied against various categories of imports from non-parties. Implementation could be tied to reciprocal obligations on the part of the parties – such as the achievement of particular greenhouse gas reduction targets, and/or the removal of trade-distorting and climate change-accelerating domestic policies, such as agricultural protection or subsidies for energy industries.

Even under these circumstances, if such trade measures were agreed *and employed*, they would represent a very severe restriction on trade, and an accompanying high welfare loss. By the same token, however, they would create a massive incentive to join and adhere to the agreement, which, after all, is the point of the trade measures. The Montreal Protocol trade measures have in fact hardly ever been used, since almost every country is now a party to the treaty.

Fairness

If the trade measures are effective in persuading or compelling countries to ratify the MEA in question, it is important that the agreement is fair. This argument has two aspects: whether the agreement itself is firmly founded in good science and a full appreciation of the issues; and whether its provisions are equitable as between countries of different types – for example, industrialized and developing. It is clearly undesirable, from the point of view of building an effective international environmental regime, if the threat or use of trade measures compels a country to join an MEA which it regards as unnecessary and which imposes excessive costs on its economy.

Once again the Montreal Protocol scores relatively highly. Although there may have been some doubts over the science and impacts of ozone depletion in the early years, there are no serious ones now. The differential phase-out schedules applied to non-Article Five and Article Five parties, and the establishment of the Multilateral Fund, with its explicit aim of meeting the 'incremental costs' of Article Five parties in complying with the requirements of the Protocol, meet the equity point. If the Fund works as it is intended, developing countries are no worse off as parties than they are as non-parties – and, indeed, they should be better off, since their adherence to the Protocol reduces the total extent and costs of ozone depletion.

This time the climate change regime also scores relatively well. The science of climate change is perhaps as good now as was the science of ozone depletion in the mid 1980s, but, clearly, the more credible it is, the stronger will be the agreement. The FCCC treats industrialized (Annex I) countries differently from developing countries. Under Article 4.2, the former group is to 'take the lead in modifying longer-term trends in anthropogenic emissions', and under 4.3, Annex II parties (basically, the OECD) are to provide financial support for developing country commitments, i.e. reporting requirements. The emission limitations and reductions agreed under the Kyoto Protocol apply so far only to industrialized (FCCC Annex I) countries. It is inconceivable that emission limitation and reduction objectives for developing countries would ever be agreed without an effective financial mechanism, whether organized through the Global Environment Facility or through some new institution. The clean development mechanism already provides a possible route for finance and technology transfer to developing countries.

Interrelationship with the multilateral trading system

Any MEA trade measures are likely in principle to be inconsistent with the MTS. As it is essentially a *proscriptive* agreement, defining what contracting parties may not do (or may do under certain circumstances), interpretation of the GATT proceeds through a case law-type approach, following rulings by dispute panels in particular cases. Although there has not yet been such a case involving an MEA, the reasoning used by GATT and WTO dispute panels in a number of trade-environment cases has been such as to suggest that MEA trade provisions might well be found to be in breach of various provisions of the GATT if such a challenge were ever to be brought. The problem is, of course, that trade measures are designed specifically to discriminate between countries based on their membership of the MEA or their environmental performance, whereas the essential basis of the MTS is to prevent discrimination in trade.

(As with other discussions of the MTS elsewhere in this book, the findings of the Appellate Body in the shrimp-turtle dispute, by implicitly permitting trade measures pursued through multilateral agreement, may modify this conclusion. It seems likely, however, that the Appellate Body's arguments would only apply to trade restrictions applied between parties to an MEA (for example, the export and import licences required under CITES) and not to Montreal Protocol-type trade measures directed against non-parties to the MEA, which, by definition, have not agreed to them.)[5]

This topic in fact became one of the most important items of debate in the WTO's Committee on Trade and the Environment in preparing its first report for the WTO ministerial meeting in December 1996. Discussion saw members putting forward proposals designed variously to define under what conditions trade measures taken pursuant to an MEA could be considered to be 'necessary' under the terms of GATT's Article XX (the 'general exceptions' article), or to establish a degree of WTO oversight on the negotiation and operation of trade provisions in future MEAs. No consensus was reached about the need for modifications to trade rules. Yet this continued threat of conflict is an undesirable, for three reasons:

1. It creates uncertainty about the legality of some existing MEAs.
2. It creates, or reinforces, the perception that the WTO regime threatens environmental sustainability.
3. It places a question mark over enforcement mechanisms in future MEAs.

Countries opposed to the aims of particular MEAs have already used the WTO-compatibility argument against the possible incorporation of

---

[5] For a more comprehensive discussion of this point, and of the WTO–MEAs debate in general, see Duncan Brack, 'Environmental Treaties and Trade' in Gary Sampson and W. Bradnee Chambers (eds), *Trade and the Environment* (United Nations University, forthcoming, 1999).

trade measures. These arguments have been raised in negotiations on driftnet fishing, on tuna conservation, on the Montreal Protocol, in the negotiations on the Biosafety Protocol in 1999, and, indeed, on the climate change regime in the run-up to Kyoto – in this case by Australia, a country which at the time appeared likely to be a non-signatory, and therefore had a direct interest in crippling any future enforcement mechanism.

Many proposals have been made for the resolution of this potential clash between international regimes. Although it is difficult to see how the CTE could agree on any of them in the foreseeable future, the issue may feature in the environmental component (if there is one) of the negotiations under the WTO's forthcoming 'Millennium Round'.

Conclusion

The trade measures of the Montreal Protocol have been a vital element in securing the success of the agreement; in principle similar provisions may have an important role to play in other MEAs. Their precise form will of course vary with the MEA in question, and in some cases they are likely to be more politically credible and technically feasible than in others. (They may be more easily applicable, for example, to the agreement controlling persistent organic pollutants than to the Kyoto Protocol.) One other general conclusion is that they should always be accompanied by effective finance and technology transfer mechanisms if the MEA is to be regarded as fair.

Ideally, the presence of trade measures should provide a sufficient incentive to result in universal participation – a conclusion which is supported by theoretical modelling suggesting that MEAs with trade restrictions evolve to one of two self-enforcing equilibrium points: universal participation or zero participation.[6] Since, in general, modern governments are not run by theoretical modellers, the *use* of any trade measures written into an MEA must at least be contemplated. In addition to matters of technical feasibility, the question of the interrelation-

---

[6] See Scott Barrett, *Climate Change Policy and International Trade* (Centre for Social and Economic Research on the Global Environment Working Paper GEC94-12, 1994).

ship with the multilateral trading system must therefore also be considered.

In purely legal terms, this could be met within the WTO (in various ways, including through an amendment to the GATT or through a separate WTO agreement on MEAs), a position for which there is some support, though also much opposition. In political terms, it is a question of both whether and how MEAs can be enforced against non-participating countries. If the objectives of the MEA are accepted as valid, and if the actions of non-participants inflict physical damage on the members of the agreement – which, in the case of transboundary or global pollution (such as climate change), they always do – then a strong case can be made for discriminatory measures directed against non-participants. Furthermore, there are a limited number of routes by which countries can affect the actions of other countries: diplomatic pressure, provision of financial and technological assistance, trade sanctions and military force. While the first two of those are clearly preferable, they have obvious limits. Trade measures are likely to continue to play a role as one component of effective environmental agreements – and should, at the very least, be contemplated as part of the evolving climate change regime.

7.3 Trade restrictions between parties

The Montreal Protocol also led to the establishment of restrictions on trade between parties in some cases. The Protocol requires parties to control both consumption and production of ODS. Since consumption is defined as production plus imports minus exports, parties must exercise control over trade if they are to satisfy their control schedules. A variety of trade restrictions have been employed, including voluntary industry agreements, product labelling requirements, requirements for import licenses (sometimes incorporating a tradable permit system), excise taxes, quantitative restrictions on imports and total or partial import bans. In addition, in response to concern over the growth in illegal trade in CFCs, an amendment was agreed at the 1997 meeting of the parties requiring parties to introduce a licensing system for all exports and imports of ODS by 1 January 2000.

It is very likely that parties to the Kyoto Protocol will develop policies which have an impact on trade. As described in Chapter 1, Article 2 of the Protocol sets out a number of activities – 'policies and measures' – which parties are encouraged to adopt in order to achieve their greenhouse gas emissions commitments, covering energy efficiency; sinks and reservoirs; agriculture; renewable energy sources (and advanced technologies in general); removal of market distortions such as subsidies; transport; and waste management. Chapters 3 and 4 describe some of the most important policies and measures which parties may adopt under this article – energy efficiency standards, carbon and/or energy taxes, the use of subsidies – which seem likely to affect international trade.[7]

Although no further details are specified in Article 2, it is not impossible that parties could claim justification from the Kyoto Protocol for measures that restrain greenhouse gas emissions from their own territories via methods that protect their own industries at the expense of importers. While paragraph 3 of Article 2 restates the principle of protection of countries from any adverse effects of any of the policies and measures that may be adopted, including effects on international trade, the wording is so general as to be fairly unhelpful for guidance in drawing up specific policies.

This is another area for a potential clash with the MTS. The WTO CTE discussions of 1995–6 frequently attempted to differentiate between 'specific measures' mandated by MEAs (such as the Montreal Protocol trade bans) and 'non-specific' measures taken pursuant to them (such as the Montreal Protocol restrictions on parties), and inevitably proposed much harsher treatment of the non-specific measures; some participants proposed banning them altogether.

The key to resolving the trade-environment debate in the context of MEAs (and more widely) lies in striking the right balance between trade liberalization and environmental protection in any given set of circumstances. While it may well be the case that trade restrictions (ac-

---

[7] The use of government procurement policies is another important area, not dealt with here, but touched on in Lucas Assunção, 'Trade Rules and Climate Change Policy: Some Issues of Synergy and Conflict', paper delivered to the Royal Institute of International Affairs conference 'Implementing the Kyoto Protocol', June 1999.

tual or theoretical) are helpful, or essential, in enforcing the implementation of a key MEA such as the Kyoto Protocol, it does not follow that *any* trade-restrictive measure that may be adopted under the treaty's aegis is desirable. In most cases, it seems unlikely that discrimination in trade would be necessary to achieving the environmental aims of the treaty. Nevertheless, in some cases it may be. This provides one further area of potential interaction between the two objectives of trade liberalization and environmental protection, and one further item for the agenda of discussions on the topic of climate change policies and their interaction with international trade.

Energy and Environmental

Programme

THE ROYAL INSTITUTE OF INTERNATIONAL AFFAIRS

**Edited by
Halina Ward and
Duncan Brack**

Trade, Investment and the Environment

ISBN 1 85383 628 1
£18.95 (pbk) 336pp.

'The debate on trade, investment and sustainable development is likely to be crucial to the outcome of the Millennium Round. I therefore warmly welcome this book which provides an invaluable guide, from widely differing viewpoints, to the essential arguments that are likely to be deployed.'

- The Rt Hon Sir Leon Brittan QC

What policies are needed in a globalized economy if environmental protection is to be secured? Can discussions on the relationship between trade, environment and investment offer genuinely 'win-win' solutions? Do the activities of transnational corporations help or hinder environmental protection? Is there a need for a new global environmental organization?

Contributors assess these crucial questions and evaluate the potential impacts of major events in the trade, investment and environment calendars: the outcome of the WTO Shrimp/Turtle dispute; the collapse of the negotiations towards a Multilateral Agreement on Investment; the WTO High Level meetings on trade and environment and trade and development; and the forthcoming Millennium Round of trade negotiations.

Contributors: Renato Ruggiero - Brian Wilson Gary Sampson - David Wakeford - Tom Burke John Gummer - David Batt - Nick Robins - Moses Adigbli - David Wheeler - Damien Geradin - Magda Shahin - Duncan Brack - Michel Potier - Reinhard Quick - René Vossenaar - Konrad von Moltke Charles Arden-Clarke - Thomas Cottier - Krista Nadakavukaren Schefer - James Cameron - Veena Jha - David Owen - Jan Huner - Kristian Ehinger - Pradeep S. Mehta - Nick Mabey - Halina Ward

Distributed exclusively in the USA and Canada by the Brookings Institution.

1999   RIIA/Earthscan

Energy and Environmental
Programme

THE ROYAL INSTITUTE OF
INTERNATIONAL AFFAIRS

Duncan Brack

ISBN 1 85383 343 6
Price £12.95 (pbk)
144pp.

International Trade and the Montreal Protocol

The Montreal Protocol on Substances that Deplete the Ozone Layer is one of the most effective multilateral environmental agreements currently in existence. Established to control the production and consumption of CFCs and other ozone-depleting chemicals, the Protocol is an important example of an agreement which places restrictions on international trade in the interests of the global environment – a feature which may become common in future treaties.

This report examines the development, effectiveness and future of the trade provisions of the ozone regime, concluding that they have contributed significantly to its success in attracting signatories and in limiting ozone depletion. Issues considered include the compatibility of the trade provisions and the GATT, trade restrictions and developing countries, and the new problems of non-compliance and illegal trade in CFCs.

Duncan Brack is Head of the Energy and Environmental Programme at the Royal Institute of International Affairs.

Distributed exclusively in the USA and Canada by the Brookings Institution.

1996   RIIA/Earthscan

Energy and Environmental

Programme

THE ROYAL INSTITUTE OF
INTERNATIONAL AFFAIRS

Jonathan Krueger

ISBN 1 85383 621 4
Price £14.95 (pbk)
160pp

International Trade and the Basel Convention

CONTENTS:
- International trade and the environment
- Transboundary movements of hazardous wastes and the Basel Convention
- Trade and the Basel Convention
- The Basel Convention and the multilateral trading system
- Developing countries and the Basel Convention
- Current issues in the Basel Convention
- Conclusions and lessons for the future

Hazardous wastes are not usually thought of as commodities traded internationally, but they are the subject of one of the most important multilateral agreements linking trade and the environment. The Basel Convention on Transboundary Movements of Hazardous Wastes and their disposal is a key environmental treaty. The Convention is best known for its role in banning hazardous wastes in developing countries. But it also has other significant implications.

This immensely readable volume examines the development, effectiveness and future of the Convention, especially its provisions for restricting trade. It analyses the compatibility between the trade provisions and the World Trade Organization, discusses the special concerns of developing countries and describes the illegal trade in hazardous wastes. It suggests ways forward for the Convention, and draws lessons from the Basel experience for other multilateral environment agreements.

Distributed exclusively in the USA and Canada by the Brookings Institution.

1999 RIIA/Earthscan

Energy and Environmental
Programme

THE ROYAL INSTITUTE OF
INTERNATIONAL AFFAIRS

Michael Grubb with
Duncan Brack and
Christiaan Vrolijk

The Kyoto Protocol:
A Guide and Assessment

ISBN 1 85383 580 3 pbk £18.95
ISBN 1 85383 581 1 hbk £45.00
384pp.

'This book... seems certain to become the foundation text for all those who
want to understand how a new chapter in international relations was opened.'
Sir John Browne, CEO, BP Amoco

'The work of the Royal Institute of International Affairs on pressing
international environmental issues has been ground-breaking, and their work
on integrating economics and the environment is particularly valuable. This
book's analysis of climate change and the challenges facing governments,
business and the wider public is in that mould: a most welcome contribution.'
Michael Meacher, Minister for the Environment, UK

'This excellent book is a much needed contribution to understanding the
history, the meaning and the relevance of the Kyoto Protocol ... Reading this
book may help negotiators to grasp what others think of the output of our work
and also to dissect the possible ways for further progress in understanding the
mitigation of climate change.'
**From the foreword by Ambassador Raúl A. Estrada-Oyuela,
Chairman of the negotiations for the Kyoto Protocol**

'An extremely perceptive analysis of past events, the ongoing debate and
future prospects related to the Kyoto Protocol. Michael Grubb's unique ability
to put even isolated developments within a larger context and relevance gives
this volume a refreshing flavour that is different from much of the literature that
is being produced on this subject ... Authoritative and candid but at all times
based on a sense of fairness and respect for equity ... an outstanding book by
a distinguished analyst and thinker.'
**Dr Rajendra Pachauri, Director, Tata Energy Research Institute, New
Delhi**

Distributed exclusively in the USA and Canada by the Brookings Institution.

1999   RIIA/Earthscan